AF652676

World Trade Organisation

Challenges and Prospects

World Trade Organisation

Challenges and Prospects

Chandra Shekhar

MD Publications Pvt Ltd
New Delhi
www.mdppl.com

Published by
MD Publications Pvt Ltd
"MD House", 11, Darya Ganj,
New Delhi-110002
Ph. : +91-11-41563325, 41562846
E-mail : **contact@mdppl.com**
Website : **www.mdppl.com**

© 2008, All rights are strictly reserved with the Publisher

ISBN : 978-81-7533-121-1

PRICE : Rs. 695.00

Published and Printed by
MD Publications Pvt Ltd at Printext,
D2/149A, Jeewan Park, Uttam Nagar, New Delhi.

PREFACE

The World Trade Organization is an international organisation designed to supervise and liberalize international trade. The WTO came into being on January 1, 1995, and is the successor to the General Agreement on Tariffs and Trade (GATT), which was created in 1948, and continued to operate for almost five decades as a de facto international organization.

The World Trade Organization deals with the rules of trade between nations at a near-global level; it is responsible for negotiating and implementing new trade agreements, and is in charge of policing member countries' adherence to all the WTO agreements, signed by the bulk of the world's trading nations and ratified in their parliaments. Most of the WTO's current work comes from the 1986-94 negotiations called the Uruguay Round, and earlier negotiations under the GATT. The organization is currently the host to new negotiations, under the Doha Development Agenda (DDA) launched in 2001.

The WTO is governed by a Ministerial Conference, which meets every two years; a General Council, which implements the conference's policy decisions and is responsible for day-to-day administration; and a director-general, who is appointed by the Ministerial Conference. The WTO's headquarters are in Geneva, Switzerland.

The WTO's stated goal is to improve the welfare of the peoples of its member countries, specifically by lowering trade barriers and providing a platform for negotiation of trade. Its main mission is "to ensure that trade flows as smoothly, predictably and freely as possible". This main mission is further specified in certain core functions serving and safeguarding five fundamental principles, which are the foundation of the multilateral trading system. Among the various functions of the WTO, these are regarded by analysts as the most important. It oversees the implementation, administration and operation of the covered agreements. It provides a forum for negotiations and for settling disputes. Additionally, it is the WTO's duty to review the national trade policies, and to ensure the coherence and transparency of trade policies through surveillance in global economic policy-making. Another priority of the WTO is the assistance of developing, least-developed and low-income countries in transition to adjust to WTO rules and disciplines through technical cooperation and training. The WTO is also a center of economic research and analysis: regular assessments of the global trade picture in its annual publications and research reports on specific topics are produced by the organization. Finally, the WTO cooperates closely with the two other components of the Bretton Woods system, the IMF and the World Bank.

The operation of the WTO dispute settlement process involves the DSB panels, the Appellate Body, the WTO Secretariat, arbitrators, independent experts and several specialized institutions. The General Council discharges its responsibilities under the DSU through the Dispute Settlement Body (DSB). Like the General Council, the DSB is composed of representatives of all WTO Members. The DSB is responsible for administering the DSU, i.e. for overseeing the entire dispute settlement process. If a member state considers that a measure adopted by another member state has deprived it of a benefit accruing to it under one of the covered agreements, it may call for consultations with the other member state. If consultations fail to resolve the dispute within 60 days after receipt of the request for consultations, the complainant state may request the establishment of a panel. It is not possible for the respondent state to prevent or delay the establishment of a panel, unless the DSB by consensus decides otherwise. The panel, normally consisting of three members appointed ad hoc by the Secretariat, sits to receive written and oral submissions of the parties, on the basis of which it is expected to make findings and conclusions for presentation to the DSB.

The process of becoming a WTO member is unique to each applicant country, and the terms of accession are dependent upon the country's stage of economic development and current trade regime. The process takes about five years, on average, but it can last more if the country is less than fully committed to the process or if political issues interfere. As is typical of WTO procedures, an offer of accession is only given once consensus is reached among interested parties.

This book provides an overview of the World Trade Organisation; in particular, it focuses on the agreements being developed at the WTO and is likely to have significant implications for libraries and information: the General Agreement on Trade in Services (the GATS) and the Agreement on Trade Related Aspects of Intellectual Property Rights (TRIPS). Furthermore, that these WTO agreements assist with this process and the furtherance of global capitalism through the WTO.

Thanks to Mr. Pranav Gupta of MD Publications Pvt Ltd, New Delhi, who supported me fully for completing this book.

Chandra Shekhar

Contents

1

WTO: Accession and Licensing

Introduction

The Country can be benefitted by the rules of the International System only if it becomes a member or is effectively represented in WTO. Accession to GATT is simple than WTO. It is complex, difficult and lengthy process. At the moment 28 countries are at various stages of the membership negotiations. Of these, 11 are transition economies that applied for accession after the collapse of central planning in the early 1990s. About half of the remainder are LDCs. China and Saudi Arabia are the two large developing countries that are in the final stage of negotiation process. Due to political considerations, there are very few countries that are neither WTO members nor applying to accede. These include Afghanistan, Iran, Iraq, Libya, Tajikistan, and Turkmenistan.

The benefits of WTO membership

Apart from the obvious benefit of participating in the activities of an institution within which the global rules for trade are set, WTO membership provides additional benefits in three main areas : (1) strengthening domestic policies and institutions for the conduct of international trade in goods and services, which is needed before accession to the WTO can be accomplished; (2) improving the ease and security of market access to major export markets; and (3) gaining access to a dispute settlement mechanism for trade issues.

Domestic policies and institutions

While there are significant differences between the institutional and policy environments of the countries applying to accede, it is remarkable how similar the opportunities and challenges of WTO membership are for individual countries or groups. When the transition economies were under central planning, the government controlled trade through ministries and state trading enterprises. The institutions governing other aspects of the international exchange of goods and services, such as intellectual property rights, standards, phytosanitary provisions and procurement were either different or non-existent. LDCs applying for accession face similar challenges in establishing the institutions needed to implement their WTO commitments. Perhaps the most important of these challenges is the introduction of laws and institutions for the operation of private enterprises and markets free from government controls, other than those explicitly provided under WTO regulations regarding, for example, health, intellectual property rights and state trading practices.

Equally important to a country's economy is the greater stability in commercial policy that comes from adherence to WTO rules and legally binding agreements. Stability is important both to domestic producers and to exporters from other countries wishing to access that country's markets. There is little doubt that adherence to the WTO provisions, for example by binding tariffs and specifying the conditions of establishment for FDI in a services agreement, improves the efficiency and productivity of acceding countries.

WTO membership also offers the opportunity for some new members to look in their relatively liberal trade regimes. While trade regimes in acceding economies vary considerably, many have established regimes with relatively low tariffs and no significant non-tariff barriers. For these countries, membership provides the opportunity to lock in these regimes by assuming legally binding obligations regarding tariff levels. This not only permits them to enjoy the benefits of liberal trade but also gives them a first line of defence against the domestic protectionist pressures that are inevitably present in all market economies.

Market access

There are two main dimensions of market access that are important to acceding economies. The first is the extension of permanent and unconditional MFN status that comes with WTO membership. At present, economies that are not Members of the WTO enjoy voluntary MFN treatment by major trading partners. But there is no guarantee that they will continue to receive such treatment. For example the US extension of MFN to Russia and several other economies in transition is contingent on these countries' adherence to the provisions of the Jackson–Vanik amendment to the 1974 Trade Act regarding freedom of emigration.

Second, there is substantial evidence that the incidence of antidumping actions (both investigations and definitive measures) is much higher against non-WTO Members than against Members. Also, for the transitional economies, some of which are considered as 'non-market economies' by major trading partners such as the EU and the US, WTO membership could help improve market access by making the processes used in antidumping cases against them more transparent.

Dispute settlement

Access to an impartial and binding dispute settlement mechanism whose decisions have a significant chance of being enforced is a very important potential benefit for the acceding economies, many of which are small and heavily dependent on international trade. The dispute settlement mechanism, in the short time since its establishment, has proven successful in providing the opportunity for a Member to satisfactorily address its grievances when the practices of other members damage to its trade. The problems developing countries face in accessing this mechanism have been noted, but membership provides opportunities that, with proper assistance, can be beneficial to new Members, especially in their relationship with large trading partners.

The accession process and strategies

The process of accession to the WTO is demanding and takes a long time for most countries. It can be divided into an introductory phase of formalities and three substantive phases. The three substantive phases involve: (1) preparation of a 'Memorandum on the Foreign Trade Regime', in which the applicant provides full details of its policies and institutions that have a bearing on the conduct of international trade; (2) the fact-finding phase; and (3) the negotiation phase. The last two phases, while conceptually separate, in practice tend to overlap. Throughout the applicant has to meet the requirements and provisions of the WTO and the demands of the existing Members. With very few exceptions the negotiations are one sided: the applicant is required to demonstrate how it intends to meet the existing WTO provisions it cannot seek to change them. Moreover the existing Members can ask the applicant to reduce the level of protection in its markets, but the reverse is not usually possible.

The formalities

The first step taken by an applicant country is to send a letter to the Director General of the WTO expressing its desire to accede to the organization. The request is then considered by the WTO General Council, which consists of representatives of all the Member countries and meets frequently during the course of the year. The General Council routinely sets up working parties with appropriate terms of reference to consider individual accession applications. The General Council nominates the chairman, but participation is open to all members of the WTO. In the case of large countries such as China and Russia, a large number of countries participate: in the case of smaller countries participation is usually limited to Quad countries, plus Australia, New Zealand, Switzerland, a few of the larger developing-country trading partners and neighbouring countries that are significant trading partners. This phase can be quite short and normally takes no longer than the time needed to find a chairman for the working party and to translate and distribute the accession request before the next meeting of the General Council.

The memorandum

The first substantive phase is the preparation of a 'Memorandum on the Foreign Trade Regime', in which the applicant explains its policies and institutions. This can be a very demanding task because of the range of issues that the memorandum has to address and the degree of detail required. The issues include much more than simply trade in goods and services although the latter, which encompasses such issues as the financial sector, insurance, telecommunications and professional services, is a large enough task in itself. The other issues include various aspects of macroeconomic policy (especially that related to foreign exchange management and controls), investment and competition policy, the protection of intellectual and other property rights, and enterprise privatization. The preparation of this report is the responsibility solely of the applicant, as is any delay in its preparation.

The greater the extent to which the memorandum is incomplete in its details or the legislation and practices described are inconsistent with the WTO provisions, the more protracted the subsequent question and answer period becomes. On some occasions Members have asked the WTO secretariat to review draft memoranda before they are circulated so as to prevent incomplete documentation from being circulated. But the secretariat does not assume any responsibility for the contents of memoranda.

Once a memorandum has been circulated to the WTO Members the accession process enters the second, often time-consuming process in which Members ask questions about and obtain clarification on the applicant's policies and institutions, based either on the memorandum or on independent evidence gathered by the Members. This typically takes several months, but in the case of Russia it took more than a year. The working party does not usually meet until the memorandum and the initial questions and answers have been distributed. The subsequent questions, answers and clarifications can occupy several working party meetings and sometimes take several years. One of the reasons why the process is so time consuming is that the review is exhaustive in its details. The applicant is requested to submit for consideration by the working party all relevant legislation on a variety of issues covered by the WTO, which is reviewed in detail for its consistency with the provisions of WTO agreements. Delays during this phase are frequent: if a member country feels that the answers submitted to a question or the actions taken to remedy an inconsistency are inadequate, it simply returns the question for resubmission.

The issues raised in each accession process vary somewhat according to the country, but some common themes emerge in the discussions especially in the case of countries in transition but often more broadly that are worth highlighting.

First, there is a general requirement for the laws and regulations of the acceding country to be in conformity with the WTO provisions. These extend far beyond the obvious, such as customs law, tariff schedules and related regulations on imports and exports. They include such items as laws on joint stock companies, the central bank and credit institutions, the licensing of economic activity, domestic taxation, regulations on food and alcoholic beverages, veterinary medicine, quarantine, patent and copyright protection, and consumer protection. The list of laws of a small country reviewed by a recent working party ran into two single-spaced pages and included than 75 laws and regulations.

Second, in the context of laws and the operation of government institutions, there are two broad issues that typically receive special attention in the case of transition economies: the degree of privatization of the economy, and the extent to which government agencies involved in the regulation of economic activity do so on the basis of transparent rules and criteria, as opposed to administrative discretion. Both of these concerns emanate from the dominant role that the state previously played in these countries' centrally planned economies. A key issue in respect of enterprises that are expected to remain state-owned is whether they operate under market conditions or enjoy special monopoly rights and privileges.

Third, there are issues that relate to the jurisdiction and capacity of national agencies to implement policies on which commitments are being made. The fundamental concern is one of governance: whether the government agencies have the authority and capacity to implement the commitments they are making in the context of WTO accession in the case of laws and regulations that concern the conduct of international trade. A related concern is the role and jurisdiction of local authorities and whether they have the right and opportunity to nullify the commitments made by the national authorities in the context of accession negotiations.

Finally, there are some issues that are particular to countries of the former Soviet Union (FSU). First, after independence most of these countries passed VAT laws under which VAT was imposed on imports from the rest of the world but not on imports from the rest of the FSU. Moreover such products were taxed at the point of origin. This is contrary to international practice and all countries acceding to the WTO are asked to change their laws accordingly. A related issue that has led to a large amount of questioning pertains to the free trade and custom union agreements signed by several FSU countries. The concern is whether these agreements are actually operative, and whether they are consistent with the WTO provisions contained in Article XXIV of GATT and Article V of GATS.

Negotiations

At some point during the question and answer phase, frequently before all the points raised by the working party have been answered, the applicant is requested to submit its initial schedule of 'offers' in goods and services. This consists of the following:

- A detailed schedule of the tariffs the applicant proposes to impose on goods and the level at which the tariffs will be bound.
- The applicant's commitments (and limitations) on maintaining access to its market for services. These include the so-called 'horizontal commitments', involving market access to and national treatment in all service sectors; and commitments and limitations in respect of the different modes of supply in the service sectors and sub sectors.
- The level of support it plans to provide to its agricultural sector relative to a base reference period (usually three representative years before the application for accession) and other aspects of its support for agricultural trade (for example export subsidies).

Once these offers have been tabled the accession process enters its final phase, which involves bilateral negotiations on proposed tariff levels and degree of openness in the service sector. These negotiations take place between the applicant and each WTO

Member who wishes to hold them. The timing of the offers varies considerably, and sometimes they are tabled very early in the question and answer phase, as for example in the case of Georgia. The bilateral negotiations often take place in parallel with formal meetings of the working party, which continues to deal with questions and answers on the foreign trade regime. The negotiating phase can also be lengthy, depending on the degree of openness the applicant proposes and the demands made by Members for market access.

When these negotiations are in the process of being finalized and the applicant has provided assurance that the legislation and institutions that will permit compliance with the WTO provisions are in place, a draft report on accession is prepared by the secretariat for consideration by the working party. This report includes the schedule of agreed commitments on goods and services. After approval from the working party, the report is forwarded to the General Council. Following a favourable decision by the General Council (usually a formality), the country is invited to sign a protocol of accession.

Progress in accession

In spring 2001, 28 working parties formally existed to consider the accession applications of prospective WTO Members. Most of these had been established for some time, and apart from few exceptions (for example those on Algeria and Laos) most of them remain active. The oldest are those on Algeria and China, which were established in 1987. On average the working parties have been in place for 67 months. If one excludes from the calculation the outliers (that is, the two oldest), those on China and Algeria, which can be considered special cases, and the three newest, which have not really started their work, the average life of the existing working parties is also 67 months.

On average it takes a little more than five years from the time the working party is established to the time that WTO membership enters into force. The eight most recent cases of WTO accession (Albania, Croatia, Estonia, Georgia, Jordan, the Kyrgyz Republic, Latvia and Mongolia) on average took more than five years, with Georgia and the Kyrgyz Republic being the fastest at a little over three years.

A number of countries are at an early stage in the negotiating process, including Azerbaijan, Bosnia-Herzegovina, Cape Verde, the Federal Republic of Yugoslavia, the Former Yugoslav Republic of Macedonia, and Yemen. Several others such as Armenia, Belarus, Kazakhstan, Russia and Ukraine have been involved in the accession process for a long time, but for various reasons are not yet close to completing it. A number of others are at a more advanced stage, with initial or revised offers on goods and services having been made, or the drafting of the working party report being under discussion (China, Chinese Taipei and Vanuatu). For most of these countries accession to the WTO is imminent, provided agreement can be reached with WTO members on the remaining points of contention.

Time Taking Process

To understand why it takes so long to accede to the WTO, one has to look more closely at the various phases of the accession process and investigate the reasons why delays may occur.

Weak follow-up

There have been several cases where a government has applied for accession and a working party has been set up, but then the applicant has not prepared a memorandum on its policies, or has done so only after a long delay. The reasons for this may include uncertainty about following through the decision to join (Nepal and Uzbekistan), or internal political conflict delaying the process (Algeria and Sudan).

In the case of Algeria, the working party was set up in 1987 but the Algerian government did not produce a memorandum until 1996. Similarly the working parties for Uzbekistan and Sudan were set up in 1994, but their memoranda of foreign trade policy were only submitted in September 1998 and January 1999 respectively.

Political issues

There are a few cases where political differences between an applicant and one or more influential WTO members have caused delays in the process. Arguably, this has to some extent been the case with China (and Chinese Taipei, which is linked to it) and the Former Yugoslav Republic of Macedonia.

Inherently time-consuming processes

The process of accession is inherently time consuming. The preparation of the memorandum presents serious difficulties to governments that lack the necessary human or material resources to address the relevant issues, which have to be analyzed in detail. In some cases there is a lack of familiarity with the concepts and legal and economic issues involved. This has been true of countries in transition and many developing countries, most of which had to seek assistance from outside experts (funded by bilateral aid agencies), the WTO itself and the World Bank. Despite this assistance, on average it took about ten months to prepare the initial memorandum (even excluding the extreme case of Algeria).

The question and answer process is also time consuming because institutional weaknesses in applicant countries can mean that it takes a long time to ascertain the consistency between the existing legislation and regulations and the WTO requirements, as well as to design and put in place the required amendments, legislation or regulations. This is compounded by the range and extent of the legislation needed, and by the fact that legislative processes are themselves time consuming. At the same time, the discussions between the applicant and the working party on points of detail can be protracted: on average it takes nine months from the time of circulation of the memorandum for the first questions and answers on it to be distributed.

The subsequent fact-finding process can also stretch over several years. In part, this can again be due to weaknesses in the institutional capacity of the applicant. The WTO secretariat can assist only in a very limited way in the accession process: the WTO budget allocation for the accession of new members is very limited and the WTO members do not devote large resources to support the accession process. The five staff in the WTO Accession Division (GATT had no explicit secretariat resources for the processing of new members) are hard pushed to service even the procedural needs and paperwork generated by the 25 or more active working parties. Finally, delays occur because fact finding about policies merges into negotiations about how existing policies need to be changed to ensure conformity with the WTO requirements.

Negotiations

The negotiating phase can be, and frequently has been, the most time-consuming phase in the accession process. The negotiations are partly about whether the applicant's policies and institutions are consistent with various aspects of the WTO agreements and partly about specific tariff bindings and commitments in agriculture and services. Delays can be caused by both sides. The applicant may be unwilling to make the necessary liberalization commitments and slow the process by, for example, not offering to liberalize its non-tariff barriers or proposing to bind tariffs at levels much higher than the current applied ones; and WTO Members may be unsatisfied with the level of liberalization proposed or unwilling to accept delays in bringing the applicant's laws and institutions into line with the WTO provisions.

Applicants' strategies and tactics

Within the rules and disciplines of the WTO, each applicant has considerable scope in respect of how restrictive or liberal its trade regime will be. There are no specific rules on the maximum level at which an applicant has to bind its tariffs, how many services it will liberalize, whether or not it will establish antidumping legislation, or how fast it will liberalize its agricultural trade. Applicants thus have a strategic choice to make during the negotiating phase: how liberal their trade regime will be, subject to the overall WTO disciplines.

One strategy that some countries have pursued in their accession negotiations is to offer the minimum degree of liberalization necessary to ensure accession. The logic of this strategy is that, for the most part, improvements in market access cannot be negotiated during accession, so it is desirable to try to maintain significant levels of protection to use as bargaining chips to obtain improved access in future negotiating rounds. Some of the countries that have used this strategy, for example China and Russia, also feel that significant levels of protection are necessary during the transition period in which the restructuring of inefficient state enterprises is undertaken. In a somewhat different vein, a number of transition economies that already have relatively low tariffs and liberal trade regimes – partly because strong devaluation of the exchange rate in the early stages of transition provided protection to domestic industry have presented initial offers that involve binding their tariffs at rates much higher than those currently applied.

Similar issues arise in services. Many transition and developing economies feel that their service sector is underdeveloped and would like to limit the commitments they make to open it up to foreign competition. This is a particular issue in areas such as financial services and telecommunications, sectors in which they frequently face requests from WTO members to establish liberal policies on commercial presence. The latter would permit foreign service suppliers to establish subsidiaries or joint ventures based on the principle of national treatment, which prohibits discrimination against foreign service providers and thus has a direct bearing on foreign direct investment.

However the minimum liberalization accession strategy can have negative effects. Individual countries, especially small developing economies, have little leverage in market access negotiations; hence any benefits they might obtain through such a strategy may be very small. At the same time, maintaining protection through relatively high tariffs and protected agriculture and services, simply means that they impose a cost on their own economies by foregoing the benefits of a more liberal trade regime, which in the first instance accrue to the country itself.

On the other hand, if countries bind their tariffs at levels higher than those currently applied and assume few commitments on agriculture and services, both of which are possible under the WTO rules, they are subject to another risk: they create an opening for domestic interests to exert political pressure for additional protection in the future.

A different strategy has been pursued by many of the transition countries that have recently become or are about to become WTO members, including Albania, Estonia, Georgia, the Kyrgyz Republic, Latvia and Mongolia. In most of these cases the governments in question have adopted a liberal trade strategy as part of the accession process, including binding tariffs at the (usually low) prevailing levels agreeing to reduce and bind tariffs at low levels as part of the negotiations; agreeing to a liberal trade regime in agriculture and services; and at an early date after accession, participating in such agreements as the government procurement code, which serves to increase competition and transparency in the operation of their markets.

The fundamental benefits of such a strategy, are economic: it provides countries with the benefits of liberal trade and investment. But it has a number of other advantages: it tends to facilitate the negotiating part of the accession process; it provides governments with political cover against domestic protectionist interests that may otherwise succeed in subverting the existing liberal trade regime; and the legally binding WTO commitments make it more difficult for future governments to reverse the liberalization. Increased protection to safeguard against serious damage to domestic industry is permitted under the WTO rules, but it is supposed to be decided on the basis of a detailed and transparent investigation to demonstrate such damage, which is then notified to the WTO and subjected to the scrutiny of other members. This is far more difficult to do than for a powerful domestic industry to seek government support to raise tariffs beyond the applied level but below the higher bound level, which a government can do almost without constraint. The point about the WTO is not that it prohibits protection, but rather that it permits it only according to certain rules, and that obeying these rules makes protection more transparent as well as more difficult to initiate and spread. The Chinese accession process, on which the bilateral negotiations have almost concluded, has combined elements of both strategies and has raised a number of additional issues that may have a spillover effect on the accession negotiations of other developing countries. First, China has used the process to stimulate and make irreversible substantial trade liberalization and more broad-based reform. Second, China, which in many ways is an economy in transition, considers itself a developing country and has been seeking to obtain the transition period and other special and differential treatment that WTO agreements extend to developing countries. The latter includes non-reciprocity, preferential market access, and different commitments and time limits for the implementation of the provisions of various aspects of the agreements, ranging from agriculture to subsidies and TRIPS. China, because of its status as a large market, has also bargained over certain aspects of its market access, such as on textiles and on issues related to its designation as a non-market economy.

WTO Member attitudes and policies

The demands made on newly acceding countries are greater, in a variety of ways, than the disciplines on existing members. Based on recent accession experiences, the following areas are ones in which Members typically request that acceding countries make commitments in excess of what many existing Members at similar levels of development have agreed to:

- **Tariffs.** Acceding countries are requested to bind all tariffs, but a large portion of the tariff schedule of many developing countries is still unbound. Ceiling bindings have been accepted, but there is pressure for the bindings to be close to the applied rates.
- **Agriculture.** In addition to binding their tariff schedule, commitments are expected on aggregate measures of support and export subsidies. As many acceding countries have not provided substantial support to agriculture, but rather penalized it, the requests they face for reductions in aggregate measures of support may not be warranted, and in any case meaningful calculation of commitments in this area is subject to serious statistical difficulties, especially for economies in transition.
- **Rules and disciplines.** Acceding countries are typically required to meet all commitments at entry (for example with regard to TRIPS, customs valuation, standards and sanitary and phytosanitary regulations), without time limits such as those available to existing members at similar levels of development, and regardless of whether institutional weakness makes it difficult for them to fulfill such commitments. Such weakness relates broadly to aspects of the operations of a market economy where it will take time to establish the proper institutional infrastructure to enable them to discharge their responsibilities properly under the WTO agreements. When such weaknesses are brought out in the negotiations, applicants are advised to seek technical assistance (available from a variety of bilateral and multilateral donors), and are asked to present details of the particular aspects of the relevant WTO provisions in which

weaknesses exist, as well as how and over what time period it proposes to remedy them.

- **Plurilateral agreements.** There is pressure on countries to examine the provisions of the plurilateral agreements on, for example, government procurement and civil aviation at the time of accession and to sign up to the agreement soon after accession.
- **Market economy issues.** The WTO agreements have no explicit requirement for member states to be market economies. On the other hand the requirement for new Members to have a fundamentally market economy is pushed de facto by existing members as part of the leverage they have in the accession process. Pressure has been exerted on all acceding countries, including China, where an explicit understanding has been reached with regard to the existence of state trading in specific sectors.

At the same time the Quad countries have been unwilling to modify their own antidumping procedures in respect of applying the designation of 'non-market economy' to transition economies that have become WTO Members. This designation is used to apply different, less transparent and potentially discriminatory practices in the determination of antidumping and, in the case of the EU, safeguard actions against imports from a number of these countries, including many former Soviet countries and China. It has been a major cause of trade friction between many transition economies and the US and EU.

The only plausible legal justification for such practices can be found in Article 2.7 of the Antidumping Agreement, which refers to the second supplementary provision in paragraph 1, which appears to permit different treatment 'in the case of imports from a country which has complete or substantially complete monopoly of its trade and where all domestic prices are fixed by the State'. Such practices were perhaps fully justified when practically all trade was controlled by state trading enterprises or ministries, and prices were fixed by the state and hence could not be taken to reflect 'normal' value. Countries in transition, however, have made great progress in introducing market forces and eliminating state trading in recent years. It would very difficult to argue that, for example, China or

Russia currently have 'a substantially complete monopoly on trade' or that all domestic prices are fixed by the state. Hence the continuation of traditional EU and US antidumping practices in the new setting appears not to be justified. However, because the antidumping provisions of GATT accept national legislation and practices as decisive, it is possible to have the odd situation where a country acceding to the WTO is still designated as a non-market economy for antidumping purposes.

Lessons from experience and issues for the future

The most important lesson gained from the accession experience is that the negotiations and their dynamics vary from case to case. Thus it is difficult to generalize. Nevertheless the cases of a number of small countries that have concluded the accession process recently suggest that the smaller the country and the more liberal its regime, the faster the accession process. This is because smaller countries realize that the costs of protection are high in small economies, and because the small size of their economies raises fewer market access problems for the major WTO members.

It is politically difficult to adopt a liberal trade strategy at accession, especially when major WTO trading partners take advantage of opportunities to limit market access that are perfectly legal under the WTO, for example maintaining high levels of protection in agriculture. While recognizing the political difficulties involved, there are strong indications that if the developing and transition economies that are currently applying for WTO membership adopt a liberal trade strategy at entry, they will maximize the benefits and opportunities for integration into the international community that WTO membership offers.

It is fair to ask whether countries should not maintain some flexibility when making their initial offers, as they are bound to face some liberalization demands by existing Members, almost irrespective of the level of protection they initially propose. However, while there is some merit to this point it should not be pushed too far. Recent experience suggests that countries that make an initial offer to bind their tariffs at levels that differ significantly from the applied levels encounter serious difficulties upon accession, although the practice is quite widespread among existing developing-country

Members, many of which have failed to bind a large portion of their tariff schedule. When such an initial offer is put on the table, working party Members may refuse to consider it or to enter into negotiations on that basis, as happened with several FSU countries and other applicants for accession. Rather they inform the country that it must submit a revised offer with bound rates that are closer to the applied ones before serious negotiations can begin.

China's accession is very unique for political and economic reasons, and lessons from it have to be drawn with extreme care. Undoubtedly China has used WTO accession to promote and lock in wide-ranging reforms. It has also been able to secure a number of transition periods (with regard to, for example, eliminating quantitative restrictions, licensing and state trading) and to maintain tariff quotas in agriculture. At the same time it has had to accept limitations on market access that other developing countries have not; for example in agreeing to be subject to product-specific selective safeguards, in accepting three more years of restrictions in the implementation of the ATC (from which it had been completely excluded) and in agreeing to be designated a non-market economy for 15 years.

Among the recently acceding countries, only China has succeeded in negotiating such transition periods, but probably has much more bargaining power than all these other countries put together. It is a moot point whether the time limits and extensions obtained by China (which were much less than it requested) are compatible with its economic interests, or whether more rapid liberalization of its trade regime would be more conducive to its long-term development. On the other hand, to the WTO Members negotiating China's accession, it is almost irrelevant what Chinese protection does to the Chinese economy. They are more concerned about the impact of such protection on their exports to the potentially large Chinese market. Hence the more exceptions a large country such as China seeks to obtain, the more WTO Members will seek to maintain provisions that inhibit full access by the acceding country's products to their markets.

While the WTO Members' insistence on the existence of a liberal commercial policy at entry is likely to serve both acceding countries long-term development interests and WTO Members' commercial objectives, their insistence on adherence to all the WTO commitments at entry and without transition periods in areas such as customs valuation, TRIPS, standards and sanitary and phytosanitary measures where obvious institutional weaknesses are present in LDCs and transition economies, raises serious problems. Applicant countries, because of their strong desire for membership, may end up agreeing to obligations that their weak institutional capacity will make difficult to implement, leaving them open to subsequent complaints. Alternatively, providing generous transition periods, while the transition periods for countries that are already Members are expiring, will create inequities between the existing and new Members. One solution to this problem may be substantially to extend some of these periods for both existing WTO low-income Members and acceding LDCs and transition economies, as the transition periods were set arbitrarily in the first place.

Sometimes, as in the case of some of the Baltic countries, accession delays have been caused not so much by problems encountered during the process per se, but by the link between WTO commitments, for example in the area of agriculture or services, and the possible future association of the applicant with the EU. For example Estonia, which has a very liberal trade regime in agriculture, had to review its WTO policy commitments in that sector in light of its interest in joining the EU and phasing in the latter's more interventionist agricultural policy. The accessions of Albania, Croatia, Estonia and Latvia were all delayed on account of EU–US disagreements over their commitments on audiovisual services.

Finally, WTO membership undoubtedly tends to create pressure to terminate non-market designation in national practices of antidumping and to permit all WTO Members to be treated the same in major markets. The experience with China, however, together with the inclusion by the EU of the Kyrgyz Republic and Mongolia in its list of non-market economies after both had become WTO Members, suggest that this anomaly is likely to continue.

It might be useful in concluding this analysis to compare briefly the WTO accession process for former Soviet countries (or any other countries for that matter) with that of membership of the Bretton Woods institutions. The speed of the former Soviet countries' accession to the Bretton Woods institutions can be explained by factors that are inherent to differences between the institutions, but it is also related to the policies and attitudes of the major developed countries, which are the largest shareholders of the Bretton Woods institutions and major actors in the WTO.

Compared with membership of the WTO, there are fewer issues on which proper legislation and regulations have to be in place before membership of the Bretton Woods institutions can be achieved. As the enactment of new legislation is a time-consuming process, this by itself can explain why membership of the WTO takes longer to achieve than membership of the Bretton Woods institutions. There is also much less negotiation on policies in the case of the Bretton Woods institutions, and certainly nothing comparable to the negotiations that take place over specific tariff bindings and commitments in services in the WTO.

An equally important factor in delays in the WTO negotiations is that the political economy of international trade policy is dominated by particular commercial interests in all countries. Thus while at the general policy level WTO Members might agree that accession of a country to the WTO is of paramount importance to their national interest - and for some large countries such as China to the very operation of the international trading system accession cannot occur until the particular commercial interests in all countries are satisfied; and that takes time.

Moreover the developed countries, whose governments play a decisive role in determining the budgets of both the Bretton Woods institutions and the WTO, ensured that large incremental resources were made available to the Bretton Woods institutions to expedite membership by the countries emerging from the ruins of the Soviet Union. In contrast, while the WTO budget for accession has been increased, the burden of preparing for accession still falls primarily on the acceding countries, supported by a number of usually uncoordinated multilateral and bilateral assistance efforts funded by aid agencies, as all countries' Trade Ministries are not mandated to help with the integration of other countries into international trade system, rather their job is to protect national commercial interests.

UNCTAD, the World Bank, the EU, Switzerland, the US and the WTO all have technical assistance programmes for various aspects of the accession process, especially the preparation of the initial memorandum. Anecdotal reports on these programmes suggest a somewhat uneven performance. Most countries have reported very helpful contributions by foreign consultants and advisors in the preparation of the memorandum. In some cases, however, the advice provided by outside experts has actually slowed the accession process, because the consultants have suggested and the countries have agreed to a bargaining strategy involving binding tariffs at high levels and limiting offers on services. At the same time, as with assistance for other purposes, there have been coordination problems among the various donors, as well as between the bilateral aid agencies providing assistance and their colleagues in the Trade Ministries negotiating the accession.

2

Developed-Country Policies

Introduction

GDP, an important determinant of the overall demand for developing-country exports, increased at a slightly lower rate than the long-term growth trends in these countries – just under 2.0 per cent for 1990–99 compared with 2.2 per cent in the 1980s and 3.0 per cent in the 1970s. On the other hand, the market access conditions for developing countries improved, partly as a result of standstills and subsequent liberalization linked to the Uruguay Round agreements and reductions in tariffs following the information technology agreement.

The actual implementation of the Uruguay Round agreements, including the information technology agreement, had not been completed by the end of the period examined, but there is evidence that access to developed-country markets was improving in many respects. Nevertheless access continued to be impeded by high trade barriers in certain sectors, such as agriculture and textiles; and while progress was made on issues such as tariff escalation, the problem persisted in certain sectors, for example textiles and leather products. Finally, as part of the Uruguay Round agreements the WTO members committed themselves to take additional steps in favour of developing countries in areas such as antidumping, the implementation of which is important to review.

Tariffs

Overall averages

The effects of the Uruguay Round agreements on the MFN tariffs of developed countries have been extensively considered in other studies, whose main findings will be summarized here. Broadly speaking the tariffs on imports of manufactures into the major industrial countries were reduced by an average of 40 per cent, from a trade-weighed average of 6.3 per cent to 3.8 per cent, with the reductions to be phased in over five years and the first installment to be put in place on 1 January 1995. Countries have reduced their tariff rates accordingly since then. Moreover in 1997, in accordance with the information technology agreement, the duty on a number of products in this sector was reduced to zero on an MFN basis.

The tariffication of various measures of support and protection in the agricultural sector resulted in substantial increases in the initial tariffs on a wide range of agricultural products in some major markets. Thus the average applied MFN rate for agricultural commodities (production weighted) in 1996 ranged from 7.9 per cent in the US to 10.7 per cent in the EU. Subsequently, developed countries were to reduce their agricultural tariffs by 36 per cent across the board, and at the same time access for agricultural products would be enhanced by reductions in domestic support measures.

The problem was that developed (and developing) countries chose to bind their tariffs at higher rates than the actual tariff equivalents during the years just before the conclusion of the Uruguay Round agreements (1989–93). For example the final bindings for the EU were almost two thirds higher than the tariff equivalents for 1989–93, and for the US they were more than three quarters higher. Binding the tariffs at such high levels allowed countries to vary their actual tariff rates according to the results they wished to achieve in protecting their domestic markets much as the EU used to do with variable levies, which have been prohibited since the Uruguay Round. The result of this so called 'dirty tariffication' has not been improved market access, merely that protection has become more transparent.

In most developed-country markets the applied MFN tariffs on other products are on average lower than in agriculture. In accordance with the liberalization measures in the Uruguay Round agreements the applied MFN tariffs on non-agricultural products range from an average of 0.8 per cent in Japan to 3.7 per cent in the US and 4.0 per cent in the EU. But the rates are higher on products of interest to developing countries. At the same time, for the Quad countries (Canada, the EU, Japan and the US), one third of all MFN tariff lines are duty free, involving a large range of products of export interest to developing countries.

Preferences

The actual tariff rates applied to imports from individual developing countries tend to be even lower than the above MFN rates, however. There are two main reasons for this: because the generalized system of preferences (GSP) further reduced the tariffs on selected commodities and countries; and because of the existence of preferential arrangements for particular countries in specific developed-country markets, for example the preferences afforded to the ACP countries in the EU market, the ones enjoyed by Mexico as part of NAFTA, and the Caribbean and Central American countries' preferential treatment in the US market as a consequence of the Caribbean Basin Initiative. In addition, individual developed countries granted preferential treatment to LDC imports following the high level meeting on trade-related measures for LDCs in 1997. For example the EU extends to the LDCs the same duty-free treatment it extends to all the ACP members, the benefits of which tend to be greater than those of the GSP.

Given the complexity of the various preferential systems, it is very difficult to assess their overall effect on the average tariffs applied to eligible developing countries. One study suggests that the GSP 'remains a valuable tool for promoting developing country exports' despite the erosion of preferences associated with the MFN tariff reduction and the increasing limitations imposed on product and country eligibility by the 'graduation' features of various programmes. This is because, when the GSP is taken into account, the average applied tariff rates decline further in major markets as the frequency of items on which duties are set at zero increases substantially doubling, for example, in the US. Notwithstanding such benefits, the GSP and other unilateral preferential schemes may offer the wrong types of 'dependency' incentives to developing countries and retard rather than promote their integration into the international trading system.

Peaks

Despite the overall decline in the average applied MFN tariffs since the Uruguay Round, there are a number of sectors and product groups in various developed countries where tariffs are substantially higher, thus limiting market access. The Uruguay Round agreements increased the tariff dispersion in some developed-country markets and reduced it in others. But in all countries there are many products and product groups in which the average MFN applied tariff level currently exceeds 12 per cent, or roughly three times the average MFN applied tariff level of developed countries. These products and groups can be defined as having tariff 'peaks'. They exist in both agriculture and manufacturing in a number of developed-country markets. But the very high rates are typically the consequence of tariffication in agriculture. The main products in which such tariff peaks can be observed are the following:

- Major staples such as meat, sugar, milk, dairy products and cereals, where the tariffication of quantitative restrictions has resulted in tariff rates frequently exceeding 100 per cent and rising, for example, to 550 per cent for rice in Japan.
- Cotton and tobacco: for similar reasons, similarly high rates are applied to these products, with the rate on tobacco reaching 350 per cent in the US.
- Fruit and vegetables, including 180 per cent for above-quota bananas in the EU, and 550 per cent and 132 per cent for shelled groundnuts in Japan and the US respectively.
- Processed food products, including fruit juice, tinned meat, peanut butter and confectionery, with rates exceeding 30 per cent in several markets and rising to 230 per cent for grape juice in the EU.

- Textiles and clothing: tariff rates are in the 12–30 per cent range for a large number of products in Canada, the EU and the US, although developing-country exports of these products are at present being restrained (but on a declining basis) under the ATC.
- Footwear and leather products, with tariff peaks in excess of 35 per cent for 10 per cent of products in Japan (rising to 160 per cent for shoes) and 17 per cent of products in Australia.
- Selected automotive and transport sector products (lorries in the US and the EU, ships and boats in Canada), with rates exceeding 20 per cent.

The GSP and other preferential schemes operated by the various developed countries tend to reduce, in some cases significantly, the tariff rates on imports of the above products from developing countries. However in almost all cases where tariff peaks are present, the sensitivity of the domestic industry to imports has resulted in the exclusion of various products from the schemes or in some type of limitation being imposed either on the amount that can be imported under the preferential rates or on the number of countries that are eligible. For example the US excludes most textile products from its GSP scheme, and the EU limits preferential margins and imposes country/sector quotas. Quota limitations also exist for non-traditional suppliers of various fruits and vegetables to the EU and in Japan's market for leather goods and footwear.

Escalation

Tariff escalation is a matter of concern for developing countries in the context of market access because it tends to increase the rate of effective protection at higher stages of processing, thereby making market access more difficult for finished manufactured products, which in turn can adversely affect developing countries' industrialization efforts. There is little disagreement that as a consequence of the Uruguay Round agreements the degree of overall escalation has decreased. But evidence from a number of sectors suggests that it is still a matter of concern.

Under the agreements the tariffs on agricultural products tended to rise. As a consequence, if one includes the tariffs on raw materials and unprocessed agriculture products in the calculation of primary products, in 1996 they were no higher than those on semi manufactures in a number of developed-country markets (the US, the EU, Canada and Norway). But this simply means that the pre-Uruguay Round calculations of tariff escalation which did not include the non-tariff barriers present in agriculture were biased upwards and the apparent improvement was less significant. At the same time, whereas the degree of overall escalation declined in all the countries studied the tariffs on finished manufactured products continued to be higher than those on semi manufactures in the developed countries, apart from the US, Japan and Australia. Furthermore, various studies of specific product chains in a number of developed countries point to continued tariff escalation in such products as processed foods (wheat flour, orange juice, vegetable oils, dairy products), clothing, leather and wood products. These findings should be treated with caution because data limitations and the continued existence of non-tariff measures in some of these product chains make it difficult to calculate the effective rates of protection. But they do suggest that tariff escalation as with tariff peaks in certain products, though reduced by the Uruguay Round agreements, continues to be an area of concern in respect of market access for developing-country exports.

Non-Tariff Measures

The Uruguay Round it is probably fair to say that the pervasiveness of core non-tariff measures in developed-country trade regimes has fallen to its lowest point in more than 50 years. By core non-tariff measures we mean the use of non-automatic licensing, quotas and tariff quotas and voluntary export restraints, as well as price control measures such as variable charges, minimum prices and voluntary export price restraints. Non-tariff measures have been drastically reduced in agriculture, where only tariff quotas continue to exist for a number of products in some of the major developed markets. At the same time the use of non-automatic licensing has reduced in all major developed-country markets, and is now primarily linked to the maintenance of sanitary and phytosanitary standards, technical standards or environmental protection. Finally, voluntary export restraints were due to be phased out by the end of 1998, and the remaining restraints in developed countries appear to be directed in significant measure against non-WTO Members. As can be seen from the table, there was a decline in the frequency of non-tariff barriers in all developed countries for all measures between 1993 and 1996. In two countries Australia and Switzerland the markets became virtually free of non-tariff barriers. In the Quad countries the total frequency ratio of border non-tariff measures ranged from a low of 1.2 per cent in Canada to 3.8 per cent in the EU. A comparison (keeping in mind the methodological limitations of some of these measures) strongly suggests that non-tariff measures are much more pervasive in developing-country than in developed-country markets. The decline in the pervasiveness of NTM reflects several factors:

- The tariffication process in agriculture, which reduced quantitative controls as well as price-related measures such as variable charges though, of course, it also increased tariffs.
- The termination of voluntary export restraints. Some restraints, for example that on sardines in the EU, have already been terminated; others were due to expire at the end of 1998. Presumably this will lead to further declines in the frequency ratios reported.
- Other ad hoc reductions of NTM.

Agriculture

The reduction of NTM in agriculture after the conclusion of the Uruguay Round does not seem to have resulted in significant improvements in market access for developing countries, for a variety of reasons. First, there were problems with the way tariffication was implemented, as discussed earlier. Second, the reduction of AMS has not affected the significant support given to products of interest to developing countries, such as sugar and dairy products. Third, despite the commitment to reduce export subsidies, these have been maintained at such high levels as to undermine the incentives provided to developing-country producers. Examples abound of the adverse effects of export subsidies on developing country-producers: subsidies in dairy products have damaged production in a large range of countries, including Brazil, Jamaica and Tanzania; subsidies on tomato concentrate have especially affected West African countries such as Burkina Faso, Mali and Senegal; support for beef has undermined efforts to increase livestock production in some of the same countries; and EU beef has come to dominate the markets of Benin and Cote d'Ivoire, for which Burkina Faso and Mali were once important suppliers. In effect, there has been far less 'real' improvement in the agricultural sector than was anticipated.

Perhaps because the agricultural agreement has not changed things as much as expected, some of the fears of net-food-importing developing countries (NFIDCs) about the possible adverse effects of the agreement have not been realized. Recall in this context the 'Decision on measures concerning the possible negative effects of the reform program on the least developed and net food importing countries'. This called for a study by the World Bank and the IMF on the implications of the agriculture agreement on food import prices for these countries and the provision of appropriate compensatory finance to deal with the problem. At the time it was considered a prime example of how 'coherence' between the WTO and the international financial institutions could be strengthened. In the event there was little evidence that the export subsidy reductions laid down in the agreement led to an increase in the import expenditures of the poorer NFIDCs, and there was no need to provide financing over and above what could be obtained through their regular facilities.

The same decision also called for the problems of the NFIDCs to be taken into account in the context of the Food Aid Convention. This convention, negotiated in 1999, stipulates that when food aid is being allocated, priority should be given to LDCs and low-income countries. Other NFIDCs can be provided with food aid 'when experiencing food emergencies or internationally recognized financial crises leading to food shortage emergencies or when food aid operations are targeted on vulnerable groups'. But there is nothing in the agreement (nor, as will be argued below, should there be) to suggest that the NFIDCs should be compensated with food aid for problems caused by trade liberalization in the developed countries.

While some of the fears about new problems proved unfounded, others were realized. These had to do with the implementation of the new SPS agreement. We discussed earlier the problems that have arisen in respect of the capacity of developing countries to develop the necessary institutional arrangements to meet their SPS-related

WTO commitments. Conforming with the set standards, along with testing and certification, account for between 2 per cent and 10 per cent of overall product costs. Hence they impose a burden on developing-country exports, even when the standards are used for legitimate reasons and the countries are able to meet them.

It has been argued of course that the SPS agreement makes developed countries' actions more transparent and ensures a degree of accountability for their actions. But the agreement may serve to legitimize developed-country actions that result in substantial problems for developing-country trade, even if the action appear to be justified, for example on health grounds. Otsuki have found that a 1998 EC regulation that raised the maximum permissible level of certain types of aflatoxin (a toxic substance) in foodstuffs and animal feed to a higher level than that required by the Codex Alimentarius, is estimated to have resulted in close to $700 million in lost revenues to African exporters of groundnuts.

At the same time fear has been expressed that developed countries may be using the SPS agreement as a form of disguised protection. This has been claimed in respect of several products: meat (Burkina Faso), fresh fruit and vegetables (Kenya), tinned tuna (Papua New Guinea) and fish (Uganda). In this regard it may not be the SPS agreement as such that is at fault, but rather its potential use to legitimize continued protection of agricultural and fishery products.

Manufactures

While the vast majority of manufactured products enter developed countries free of non-tariff controls, such controls are pervasive in a few sectors, including clothing in the US, EU and Canada, and silk and man-made fibres in Japan. This largely reflects the continuing influence of the ATC, which at present constitutes the main remaining NTM impeding access to developed-country markets.

Under the terms of the agreement the integration of the textile and clothing sector into GATT (for example the elimination of quantitative restrictions that would otherwise not be permitted by GATT) is taking place in stages. Stage 1 involves the integration into GATT of 16 per cent of products in four specific categories upon the entry into force of the WTO agreement. Stage 2, involving the integration of another 17 per cent by volume, started on 1 January 1998. Stage 3, involving 18 per cent, will start on 1 January 2002, and the balance will be integrated on 1 January 2005. In parallel, specific quotas are being eliminated as a consequence of the integration process, and the remaining ones are being enlarged at specified rates.

In 1997 the Textile Monitoring Body, set up to monitor the implementation of the ATC, conducted a review of the liberalization steps members had taken during the first stage of the implementation of the agreement, the plans for the further liberalization of textiles and clothing during the second stage of implementation and other aspects of the implementation of the agreement including the use of a transitional safeguard mechanism, and special provisions for least-developed countries and cotton-producing exporters.

The Textile Monitoring Body's review revealed that the four major developed country-members that maintained restrictions (the US, the EU, Canada and Norway) had met their commitments in terms of liberalizing 16 per cent of their 1990 imports by volume (of the appropriate textile and clothing categories) during the first stage and their planned integration of another 17 per cent of 1990 imports by volume during the second stage. However they had done so by including low-value products (which they had the right to do to under the ATC). As a consequence the liberalization of textiles during the second stage will only amount to between 18 per cent and 29 per cent (in value terms) of the 1990 imports, leaving the bulk of the liberalization for the end of the period. In addition the review suggested that the quotas would actually be eliminated on only a few products in stages 1 and 2 and the annual growth rates for the remaining quotas would be small. Thus while implementation of the ATC can be viewed as being consistent with the legal requirements, the manner in which it has been implemented raises the question of whether developed countries will find it possible to honour their commitment to integrate all of their textile and clothing sector into the mainstream GATT rules by 2009.

As the value of textile and clothing imports liberalized in countries with quotas under the agreement had been small, the review expressed concern about the likelihood of subsequent elimination of trade barriers by the developed countries (ibid.). As the liberalization of clothing and textiles was an important aspect of the overall commitments and concessions made by developing countries in the Uruguay Round agreements, doubt about the willingness of the developed countries to undertake the adjustment steps needed for the further integration of the textile and clothing sector into GATT is tending to cloud the atmosphere for negotiations in other areas.

Trade remedies

The evidence shows that the frequency of antidumping and countervailing actions (as well as other price-related controls) in developed countries declined significantly during 1994–97. Several developed countries (Japan, Switzerland and Norway) used no such measures at all; while in other countries (the EU and Canada) the frequency of their use fell to less than 1 per cent of the total tariff lines.

This evidence is corroborated by a detailed analysis of antidumping actions by developed countries (based on the WTO Antidumping Database). It shows that the annual average number of antidumping investigations initiated by developed countries fell from 160 cases in 1989–93 to 95 in 1994–97, although they increased in 1997 after declining for four consecutive years. It is too early to say whether this marked the beginning of a series of actions. It is also worth noting that the share of developed countries in antidumping investigations fell to less than 50 per cent of total investigations in the later period – that is, in the later period it was developing rather than developed countries that initiated the majority of antidumping investigations.

Most of the developed-country antidumping investigations and definitive measures against developing countries have been directed at higher- and middle-income developing countries (often the same countries that have themselves made increasing use of antidumping measures) and non-WTO members. Bangladesh is the only LDC to have been subjected to antidumping investigations and definitive measures on three occasions.

The major product groups that are the object of anti-dumping investigations are much the same for developed as for developing countries. It shows that basic metals, chemicals, plastics, and machinery and electrical equipment account for the bulk of antidumping investigations in both developed and developing countries, although the emphasis naturally tends to differ from country to country. These four sectors together accounted for more than two thirds of all antidumping investigations world-wide over the decade 1987 to 1997.

Finally, it is important to recall that during the Uruguay Round, and in the context of the Agreement on the Implementation of GATT Article VI on antidumping, the developed countries committed themselves to giving special regard to the special situation of developing-country members when considering antidumping measures under the agreement. The possibility of using the constructive remedies provided for in the agreement should be explored before applying antidumping duties that will affect the essential interests of developing-country members.

There is little guidance on how this article should be implemented, particularly in respect of the way in which the special situation of developing-country members should be taken into account. The article does not appear to commit developed countries to do anything more than make use of the constructive remedies mentioned in the agreement before applying antidumping duties. But presumably they would have to do this in all cases, not only those involving developing countries. In practice the results have been mixed. On the one hand the overall use of antidumping action by developed countries and the total number of cases brought against developing countries have declined since the Uruguay Round. On the other hand the proportion of investigations in which developing countries have been affected has been much higher than the share of developing countries in world exports.

The ratio of the two shares, R_{ad}, should be interpreted with care because the proportion of investigations may not accurately reflect the actual quantities of exports affected. The R_{ad} for investigations of developing countries had a value of 1.6 compared with 0.6 for the developed countries in that period. This means that developing countries were more than twice as likely to have their imports affected by an antidumping investigation (relative to their share in international trade) than developed countries.

The situation has not changed since the WTO came into being. It shows that the R_{ad} values have basically remained the same for both developed and developing countries, but the values for the former have continued to be much lower than those for the latter. The table also shows a very large incidence of antidumping actions against non-WTO members, especially the so-called 'non-market economies', whose share of antidumping investigations was disproportionate to their share of world trade. Indeed, controlling for the value of total exports, an antidumping investigation over the decade in question was at least four times more likely to be directed against a product from a non-WTO, non-market economy than a product from a developed-market economy. In this regard the situation of non-WTO, non-market economies (essentially China and the countries of the former Soviet Union) deteriorated after the establishment of the WTO. In the period 1995–97 their exports were targeted for antidumping investigations six times more frequently than exports from developed countries.

The differences between country groups become even more pronounced when R_{ad} values are calculated for definitive antidumping measures. In the 1995–97 period, definitive measures were five times more likely to be taken against developing-country compared with developed-country exports; and they were even more likely to be taken against non-WTO members, especially countries classified as non-market economies. These countries, which accounted for less than 7 per cent of world exports, were affected by about a third of the definitive antidumping measures taken in 1995–97.

It has been argued that the reason for the disproportionate share of investigations against transition economies and developing countries is that 'the latest arrivals in the world markets tend to price their exports competitively, because otherwise they cannot capture market share from incumbents'. It suggests that other factors may also be at play: the very high incidence of antidumping actions against non-WTO members that are classified as non-market transition economies by the EU and the US, as compared with the incidence of investigations and definitive actions against transitional economies that are already WTO members, suggests that countries may feel less constrained about taking action against non-WTO countries. And with respect to so-called non-market economies, there is evidence to suggest that the procedures used tend to be more opaque and may well lead to a greater incidence of definitive findings than those used against other economies.

What can be concluded from this analysis of the prevalence of antidumping actions against developing countries as an indicator of market access to developed-country markets? There appears to have been an improvement in recent years because in general fewer antidumping actions have been taken by developed countries, but the developing countries' share of these actions, taking account of the value of their exports, has not changed and tends to be disproportionately high for investigations and even more so for definitive actions. This reflects a somewhat mixed response by the developed countries to their commitment to give special regard to the situation of developing countries. Similarly, there is no evidence that the Article 15 provision on using constructive remedies before applying antidumping duties on imports from developing countries has been employed.

Least developed countries

The international community has made a special effort to address the market access problems faced by the LDCs. For example, as noted above, only one LDC has been subjected to antidumping action by a developed country. Since the 1997 high level meeting on LDCs, developed countries (and other developing countries) have made additional preferential market-access commitments to LDCs.

Given the attention that the international community devoted to the question of integrating LDCs into the international trading system, it is worth noting that partly as a result of the composition of their exports and partly as a consequence of the special preferences these countries typically enjoy in developed countries the average tariff rates they face in developed-country markets are generally much lower than those levied on other countries.

Overall it is estimated that 80–90 per cent of the value of LDC merchandise exports have duty free access to the main developed-country markets. It has also been estimated that in 1995 the average unweighted tariff applied to the LDCs' main exports to seven developed-country markets (the Quad countries plus Australia, Norway and Switzerland), taking account of all the preferences they enjoy, was 1.8 per cent, substantially less than the average tariff of 3.6 per cent faced by all developing countries. The average is set to decline further as a consequence of improvements since the high-level meeting. At the same time the tariffs levied in other developing-country markets on LDC products are much higher – 14.5 per cent.

The main reason why the tariff rates for LDCs are so low is that the bulk of their exports are primary commodities on which tariffs are low or absent, and because of the extensive preferences they enjoy in major markets. Even so, about 10 per cent of LDC exports to developed countries face tariffs of more than 5 per cent and there is some tariff escalation. The main product sectors in which high tariffs are charged are agriculture, clothing and footwear, that is, much the same sectors that are important to other developing countries. For a number of products (beef, asparagus, cigarettes, processed wood, clothing and footwear), amounting to about 10 per cent of the LDCs' total exports, tariffs in the seven developed-country markets noted above range from 5 per cent to 15 per cent.

The incidence of non-tariff measures against imports from LDCs is difficult to measure. The only available estimate is based on a frequency distribution of controls on 112 leading LDC export products. This shows that LDCs face a probability that about 6 per cent of the 112 products will be subject to some type of formal non-tariff measure or control such as licensing, quotas, tariff quotas and so on in developed-country markets, and 16 per cent in developing-country markets. These 'formal' non-tariff barriers do not include barriers or limitations that are less formal but may be of even greater importance in constraining LDC exports because of the acute institutional inadequacies in these countries. These include the necessity of meeting the SPS requirements for food and fish products, eco-labelling requirements and the difficulty of taking advantage of preferential arrangements because of complex rules of origin.

In sum the market access problems for LDCs mainly concern a few particular products and tend to be greater for developing-country than developed-country markets. At the third WTO ministerial meeting there were indications that developed countries might be prepared to go further in extending voluntary preferences to these countries, perhaps even commiting themselves to duty-free access for all LDC exports as part of new round. Such commitments are relatively easy to make in political economy terms, as LDCs account for a very small faction of developed-country imports in most product categories. As a consequence LDCs may not have to offer any new liberalizing commitments in order to obtain improved market access.

Services

As is the case with developing countries, there are no systematic investigations of developed-country policy on trade in services and the implications of the restrictions they impose on potential exports from developing countries. The impression is that their overall policies on service imports are more liberal than those of the developing countries because they have made more commitments on liberalization under GATS. But when it comes to the movement of natural persons they tend to be more restrictive than developing countries regardless of sector. Liberalization in this area would be of considerable benefit to developing countries because of the latter's comparative advantage in labour-intensive services across all modes of supply. In addition, in maritime services international competition is extremely limited and there are serious constraints deriving from national legislation that actively discriminates against foreign suppliers, as in the US.

Movement of natural persons

While some progress has been made with regard to the movement of qualified professionals to work abroad, developed-country restrictions inhibit increased service earnings for developing countries through this mode of supply. The commitments on trade in services tend to emphasize the regulation of commercial presence, which is important for foreign direct investment, rather than 'mode four' involving movements of natural persons.

There are quantitative restrictions on the number of visas issued per year, and the qualification and licensing requirements of professional organizations formally discriminate against foreign qualifications. Still other barriers involve wage-matching requirements whereby the wages paid to foreigners must be the same as those paid to nationals and the provision of local training.

The commitments on the movement of natural persons primarily involve intra-corporate transferees, business visitors and, to a lesser extent, independent professionals, including those providing services under a service contract. A large number of countries impose an economic needs test. This typically involves judgements by government agencies, based on non-transparent criteria (market conditions, the availability of local service providers and so on), as to which foreign service providers to permit and which to refuse. Indeed, of the 54 countries that have made their commitments subject to a needs test, only three have revealed their criteria for the test. Frequently the result is to nullify access commitments involving 'mode four' service supply.

There are many sectors in which developing countries have a comparative advantage, usually based on labour costs, and would benefit from developed-country liberalization, particularly in respect of software development and construction services. The former is an area where developing-country exports, for example from India, have been expanding very rapidly in recent years. Many of these exports involve onshore delivery because of the need for continuous contact between client and programmer. While technological and managerial innovations may cause the share of onshore delivery to decline, with increases coming mainly from cross-border trade, the increased software demand by developing countries may be so high as to necessitate the further liberalization of 'mode four' restrictions. Similarly, several developing countries, especially in Asia, have the capacity to export construction services, based on their comparative advantage in labour-intensive activities, but are constrained by developed-country restrictions on the movement of persons.

Maritime services

Efforts to reach agreement on this sector during the Uruguay Round failed in 1995–96, and the negotiations were suspended with a view to resuming them in the wider context of the negotiations starting in 2000. This should be a major area of interest for developing countries in the service negotiations.

Shipping continues to be dominated by cartels known as shipping conferences. These cartels fix prices and pursue other collusive activities in the substantial proportion of maritime services they control and they are often exempt from antitrust law in developed countries. The effect they have had in raising transport costs to poorer developing countries, especially in the case of low-volume, long-distance shipping to Africa and poorer island economies, would not even be offset by further tariff liberalization: the shipping margins on merchandise trade in Sub-Saharan Africa exceed 6 per cent compared with the OECD tariffs (after preferences are taken into account) of less than 2 per cent (ibid.). Liberalization in this sector, which would lead to increased competition and reduced margins, would be of great importance to many of the small WTO Members.

Implications for market access negotiations

Despite the many complaints by developing countries about the market access conditions they face in developed countries, it is clear that the situation has improved since the Uruguay Round. However a number of problems remain. Some of them relate to how the Uruguay Round commitments have (or have not) been implemented by developed countries. Others relate to issues that the Uruguay Round did not address fully or well and need to be taken up in a new Round of multilateral negotiations.

Agriculture

While the Uruguay Round provided a major step forward by bringing the agricultural sector under the disciplines of GATT, very substantial protection continues to exist in the form of controls and interventions that encumber international trade. The above analysis suggests that the different developing countries face different situations and challenges in their agricultural sectors, which may well result in different groups of developing countries emphasizing different issues in the ongoing WTO negotiations. First, a number of developing countries (members of the Cairns group) have relatively low agricultural protection but are major exporters of agricultural commodities. These countries face two major challenges in expanding their agricultural exports: the continued presence of high tariffs and substantial AMS by developed countries, which restrict market access; and developed-country export subsidies, which make it difficult for them to compete in third-country markets.

A second group of countries includes the traditional net-food-importing developing countries (NFIDCs) and others with substantial agricultural protection. These countries are concerned that the reduction of export subsidies by the developed countries will increase their import bills. However there is little evidence that these countries have been harmed by the reductions implemented so far. Indeed the main problems they face derive from the fact that the continuation of large subsidies and protection in the developed countries is undermining production incentives in these developing countries.

Even so, it is appropriate to consider what will happen if developed-country export subsidies do decline in the future, and what the proper international response should be. The main problem concerns the adverse short-term effects that the elimination of trade-distorting measures may have on poor NFIDCs, although these are likely to be outweighed in the longer term by world-wide efficiency gains. Actually the short-term effects are likely to spread out over time as the distortions are bound to be phased out rather than eliminated at once. And it would be very difficult to isolate the impact of the resulting price increases from other factors, including the developing countries' own policies. It is for this reason that the IMF did not provide automatic financing from its Compensatory Finance Facility (CFF) for cereals, but drawings from the CFF were included in the IMF programmes for individual countries. But there is nothing – nor should there be automatic about the assistance provided. Indeed if a need is shown to exist the international response should not be limited to food aid but should extend to general purpose financing on appropriate terms. The latter would be better than food aid, which is frequently tied to procurement from a particular donor and determined by food stock availability in the donor country rather than by the needs of the recipient.

The new Food Aid Convention should prove of great assistance to developing countries as a whole, and could help in a small way with some of the food security problems many face, but it is not a substitute for the further liberalization of agricultural trade – indeed it should be viewed as a supporting element of such liberalization. Reduced protection in developed-country markets will improve the market access prospects of both existing and potential exporters; while reduced developed-country export subsidies will lessen the international market distortions that impede the expansion of developing-country agricultural production, and reduction of their own agricultural protection (as part of a broader reduction of protection) will stimulate efficiency through improved allocation of domestic resources.

Manufactures

The policy issues surrounding the protection of trade in manufactures can be divided into three distinct areas: tariffs, non-tariff measures and trade remedies.

Tariffs

There is mounting support by several countries both developed and developing for tariff reduction (outside agriculture) to be made part of future WTO multilateral negotiations. Developing countries have been concerned about tariff peaks and escalation in developed-country markets for some categories of manufactures. The above analysis shows that there are peaks in agricultural commodities and processed foodstuffs (which should be a subject of the negotiations in agriculture), textiles and clothing and a few other sectors, including leather products and cars. The analysis also shows that applied tariffs for manufactures are on average higher in developing countries than in developed countries. This is even more the case when bound rates are compared, and many developing countries have not bound a significant proportion of their tariffs on manufactures.

Further tariff reduction in manufactures would benefit all countries because of the efficiency losses caused by the protection of the country imposing it. As noted, this is likely to involve pressure for the developing countries to take considerable action in this area because their tariff levels are much higher than those of developed countries. They will also be under pressure to reduce ceiling bindings, as well as to bind a significant portion of the tariffs that remain unbound in many countries. The developed countries have already reduced their tariffs on most manufactures, and those which remain are concentrated in a few sensitive sectors. There will be opposition by some major developed countries for tariff reductions in these areas, especially in the case of textile and clothing, since with the implementation of the ATC, tariffs will be the sole means of protection available to this sector.

As there are few such sectors outside agriculture, developing countries will need to seek a formula for reducing tariffs that will permit them to exchange reductions in their tariffs on a broad range of products for reductions in the peaks that occur in the manufacturing sector of developed countries. Finally, as trade in manufactures between the developing countries is rapidly expanding, they would benefit significantly from mutual reductions in those tariff barriers which affect their exports to other developing-country markets.

Non-tariff measures

As there are few remaining formal NTM in the developed countries, the key issues for developing countries are for the commitments under the ATC to be implemented and for NTM not to be imposed under the guise of any other rules or arrangements. One way in which this might occur is through the application of discriminatory rules and practices under the agreements on SPS and TBT. The way to guard against this development is to scrutinize the actions of developed countries to ensure appropriate implementation of the relevant agreements. But while textiles and clothing actions are being monitored systematically by the Textile Bureau, there is no similar agreement for SPS measures and TBT – areas in which many developing countries have a limited institutional capacity, which may constrain their ability to scrutinize the consistency of developed-country actions.

Trade remedies

Many developing countries have decried the fact that developed countries have done next to nothing to implement the 'best efforts' provisions of the Uruguay Round agreement on antidumping. Instead of providing developing countries with more favourable treatment, developed countries have taken proportionately more antidumping actions against developing countries than is warranted by their share of world trade. At the same time, as noted above, many developing countries have abandoned the use of non-tariff measures to protect their manufacturing sector and are using antidumping and to a lesser extent safeguard measures instead. The only way forward on this issue is for developed and developing countries to agree to a tightening of the WTO antidumping agreement provisions in the context of a new Round of multilateral trade negotiations. It is difficult to say whether the political will exists to move forward in this area in either group of countries.

Services

The main way in which developed-country restraints are damaging developing countries is through 'mode four' limitations on the movement of natural persons. This is adversely affecting developing country interests in all sectors, but especially in software development and construction. In addition, developed-country restrictions on maritime services are imposing a severe burden on a number of developing countries, especially small island economies and others located far from the main markets.

On the other hand the developing countries have not liberalized their own services trade in many sectors; or if they have, they have not made binding commitments. As in tariffs, this again appears to be an area in which negotiations on further multilateral liberalization may yield large dividends for developed and developing countries alike.

Least developed countries

The international community especially the developed world has devoted an extraordinary amount of attention to the problem of market access for the LDCs. This attention is out of proportion to the contribution that concerted action in this area is likely to make to the integration of these economies into the world trading system. This is because access for these countries' exports is largely free already, and the main constraints on integration derive from institutional capacity and other supply-side factors. Moreover the major problem is gaining access to the markets of other developing countries, not those of developed countries.

Nonetheless attention to LDC market access issues has become symbolic for developing countries that seek evidence of developed-country support for developing-country issues in the context of a new Round of negotiations. The issue has become a symbolic gesture of a different kind: in developed countries market access is already relatively free and the products in which LDCs account for even an identifiable share of developed country markets are few and far between. Thus, it would be relatively easy for developed countries to make this symbolic gesture as it would not have significant impact on major domestic protected interests.

Nevertheless it is symptomatic of the developed countries' reluctance to open up their markets in sensitive areas that the several efforts to reach agreement on providing the LDCs with completely duty-free and quota-free access have failed. The main difficulties arise in agriculture and textiles, the same sectors identified as posing problems for all developing countries. In late 2000 the European

Commission proposed duty- and quota-free access for all but three commodities (bananas, rice and sugar), phased in over three years. The proposal ran into predictable protectionist opposition by EU farming interests as well as non-LDC exporters from the ACP countries, which would lose some of the preferences they enjoy in the EU market. This resulted in a modification of the original proposal and extension of the phase-out of the quotas to 2006–8. It is important for the international community to agree to a similar gesture as that made by the EU. This would be as important for the improved atmosphere it would create during negotiations as it would for the new producers of the few products that would gain access to developed-country markets as a result. But it is also essential that this gesture be accompanied by action on the part of other developing countries to facilitate LDC access to their markets. Such liberalization might actually prove even more important than other measures aimed at boosting LDC exports.

3

Liberalizing Trade in Services

Introduction

Many observers were critical of the structure of the General Agreement on Trade in Services (GATS). They argued that schedules are hard to interpret and would not generate a powerful momentum for future liberalization of markets. The "positive" list approach toward scheduling commitments was perceived as an opaque instrument (it is difficult to know what is not liberalized). The sectoral focus (illustrated by specific annexes for financial services and telecoms) was seen as a danger because it limited the potential for intersectoral trade-offs and concessions by GATS members.

Developments subsequent to the Uruguay Round have given some cause for optimism but also provide cause for concern. On the positive side, the sectoral approach worked better than expected. Two agreements on key services sectors (financial services and basic telecoms) were successfully negotiated. Although these agreements introduce only a limited dose of liberalization, that they were concluded at all suggests the critics may have been too pessimistic. The pessimists can point to the failure of efforts to conclude sectoral talks to liberalize maritime transport (under GATS) and to negotiate a Multilateral Agreement on Investment (MAI) (under the Organization for Economic Cooperation and Development). Among the many disturbing aspects of the MAI negotiations was that it revealed that a "negative" list approach to scheduling commitments is not necessarily a much better way of dealing with complex barriers to competition: the lists tabled by MAI negotiators were so long that they tended to make the general MAI disciplines irrelevant. The MAI experience illustrates that although there is value in transparency, this alone is not sufficient to move a liberalization agenda forward. It needs to be supported by domestic political forces that favor the pursuit of liberalization. The existence of such a domestic consensus was a major factor behind the successful conclusion of the GATS basic telecom talks.

In many countries attempts to liberalize services during the Uruguay Round were not accompanied by a wide and lively debate on national interests and objectives. Often negotiating positions were largely driven by specific industry interests. This was one factor underlying the limited liberalization that was achieved rational "status quo bias" prevailed. After its inception, GATS continued to attract little public attention. Its provisions, let alone its existence, remain relatively unknown or little understood even among those who have an interest in the functioning of the trading system (multinational business). No major disputes about the implementation of the agreement have been brought forward. This suggests the agreement is not perceived as particularly relevant to the various stakeholders (business, consumer groups). At the same time, there is a strong sense of disquiet in many countries about the impact on national welfare of multilateral liberalization commitments.

New negotiations on services are due to be initiated in 2000 as called for in the Uruguay Round Agreement. Members of the World Trade Organization will have to determine how and what to negotiate. The MAI experience must be internalized, but how to do this is not clear, especially given vociferous opposition by some influential nongovernmental organizations to strengthening the trading system. Meanwhile, there is a wide recognition among the business community and officials that the status quo is not an acceptable option, simply because the existing schedules of commitments in the GATS are not particularly useful. The correspondence between what is scheduled and the effective barriers to trade and investment that are in force is rather loose, to say the least. The question of how to proceed on services is particularly acute for developing countries. Almost all governments increasingly recognize the vital role that an efficient and vibrant service industry plays in the process of economic and social development (certain services are basic inputs or components of the economic infrastructure, whereas other services can be a provisional shelter useful for social stability).

This chapter discusses how the coming WTO negotiations might best be used to help achieve national economic objectives.

General Equilibrium and Pursue Neutrality

Governments intervene in markets for a number of reasons: to provide public goods; to redistribute income in the pursuit of equity objectives; and to protect and support favored industries or activities. Such support is provided among other ways through trade protection and fiscal incentives (tax concessions, subsidies). The tariff peaks and the tariff "escalation" found in most national tariff schedules reflect the desire to favor certain industries over others. As a result, effective rates of protection can be very high or very low negative rates of effective protection are not rare that is, activities may be taxed rather than supported. It provides general evidence on the survival of tariff escalation and dispersion after more than forty years of GATT-based rounds of negotiations to reduce barriers to merchandise trade.

The economic justification for government intervention to favor certain economic activities over others generally rests on the existence of market failure, that is, externalities. While the theoretical case for intervention is clear cut, in practice the interventions observed in most countries to favor some industries over others are not aimed at offsetting market failures. Instead, they simply reflect the outcome of political processes and rent-seeking (directly unproductive profit-seeking) activities. From a national welfare perspective such selective intervention is costly, leading economists to suggest that a good rule of thumb for policy is to establish a level playing field in the sense that incentives to engage in different types of economic activities are neutral. While government should intervene to ensure that firms and households take into account the negative externalities that are created by their activities (through pollution taxes, zoning restrictions, and so on) and can benefit from positive spillovers (for example, education, infrastructure), these are non-industry-specific types of actions. At the firm or industry level the incentive structure should be neutral.

Table 3.1. Nominal Rates of Assistance via Trade Policies, 1992

Item	Advanced industrial economies	Newly industrialized economies	Low- and middle-income economies
1992			
Agriculture and processed food	39	43	7
Other primary and manufacturing industries	3	8	12
Post-Uruguay Round			
Agriculture and processed food	33	33	6
Other primary and manufacturing industries	2	6	11

The rationale for this is largely a political economy one. Although in theory industry-specific intervention might be justified on a variety of "strategic" grounds, as was pointed out by Friedrich Hayek more than fifty years ago, in practice governments will lack the information necessary to realize the potential gains. If parties recognize that in addition to the information problem, political imperatives and rent-seeking will inevitably induce governments to diverge from "optimal" interventions, a strong case can be made for pursuing neutrality as a fundamental rule of policy toward industries.

Many governments around the world are far from achieving this policy prescription. Although in practice it will be impossible to achieve fully, neutrality is a useful lens through which to assess status quo policies and identify reform priorities. One reason is that neutrality requires an economy-wide or general equilibrium framework to be used that considers the impact of one industry-specific policy on the economy at large. The absence of such a framework often results in highly non uniform patterns of protection for industries that are detrimental to the long-term growth prospects of the economy. An example is the treatment of agriculture in many developing economies. Policies such as manufacturing protectionism and overvalued exchange rates tend to discourage farm production. Within the farm sector, the developing countries discourage exporters more explicitly than farmers who compete with imports. The emerging markets that were embroiled in financial crisis in the late 1990s are another illustration. There is a strong parallel between the steel crisis in Europe in the 1970s and the banking crisis in Asia in the 1990s. In both cases, one sector remained highly protected during a period in which substitute goods or services were being liberalized. In Europe, protection for aluminum and other substitutes for steel were gradually reduced at a time of decreasing transportation costs; similarly in the banking case, short-term capital flows were being liberalized when the electronic "transportation" costs of moving funds was declining rapidly, whereas inward foreign direct investment (FDI) in the financial services industry in many Asian economies remained restricted.

These examples show the need for a comprehensive as opposed to a piecemeal approach toward liberalization and reform in order to reduce the dispersion in the incentives to undertake investments across sectors and activities. This is not to deny the role governments must play in redistribution and the provision of public goods or to deny that in the pursuit of these activities governments will invariably affect economic activity. Central decision makers have become increasingly aware of the benefits of a "general equilibrium" approach in terms of improving resource allocation incentives. For example, growing recognition that differences in domestic indirect tax rates can be damaging has led to a reduction in the dispersion in tax rates. A relative shift away from subsidies has also occurred, motivated by the same factor of distrust of selective public actions (of course, driven also by budgetary constraints).

Of particular importance in the context of the prospective WTO negotiations is that a "general equilibrium" assessment should cover both goods and services to consider interaction effects. Actions taken in services markets can affect competition in goods markets and vice versa. Restrictions on competition in European car distribution as a means to support the European Community voluntary export restraint agreement with Japan on cars are one example. Similar effects may be caused by legislation allowing exclusive distribution or sole agency, or by restrictions on parallel imports of branded goods. These practices can prevent the benefits of trade liberalization being realized by consumers instead, the effect may be to transfer what was previously captured as tariff revenue by the government to the private interests that control distribution of imports. Such indirect effects are not limited to manufactures: a major trade reform program undertaken by India in the early 1990s, which reduced import-weighted average tariffs from 87 percent in 1991 to 27 percent in 1996, induced a disappointing agricultural supply response because of policies that restricted competition in the provision of key inputs such as credit, transport, storage, and communication services.

Achieving Greater Uniformity

The process of liberalizing trade in goods through reciprocal negotiations under GATT auspices has been successful because the intrinsically mercantilist behavior of trade negotiators (who focus exclusively on obtaining better access to the export market for their national industries, using domestic trade barriers as negotiating coin) was consistent with (and led to) the economically sound policy that focuses on the benefits for the domestic economy from cheaper imports and an improved allocation of resources that better reflects comparative costs. Because negotiating coin had to be expended to obtain better access to export markets, the process led to a gradual move toward the globally efficient outcome free trade. Each GATT round led to successive reductions in foreign tariffs that were profitable for domestic exporters and decreases in domestic tariffs that were beneficial to domestic consumers. The latter were made feasible because export interests were willing (required) to support liberalization in domestic political markets.

Of course, the GATT focus on reciprocity is not ideal by any means. Abstracting from the nontrivial opportunity costs of maintaining protection, it results in a non uniform pattern of protection. Uniformity in protection across activities is a key element for getting the most out of trade liberalization. In this perspective, the frequent focus on the "average" tariff by countries in trade negotiations is virtually meaningless: even if the average is low, the real costs of protection can be high if the dispersion of tariff rates across commodity groups is large. This is because the consumer deadweight losses from protection increase more rapidly than the level of protection and because distortions in terms of resource allocation tend to be more harmful as the dispersion of tariffs increases (such costs are a square function of the tariff level in the case of linear demand and supply curves). Account should also be taken of the administrative costs of non uniform tariffs, rent-seeking, and corruption. Notwithstanding these caveats, GATT rounds resulted in greater uniformity: as tariffs were brought down, they also became increasingly similar. The mercantilist approach of negotiators also helped to reduce the dispersion of tariffs directly: some of the negotiating formulas that were developed targeted high tariffs more than low tariffs in an attempt to increase access to more protected markets more than proportionately. Reciprocity worked well because two conditions were satisfied: tariffs constituted the dominant barrier on trade in goods, and most of the other major non tariff barriers (quotas, antidumping measures, and so on) are not too difficult to "translate" in tariff terms. As a result, the value of "reciprocal concessions" associated with tariff or non tariff barrier reduction has not been too difficult to estimate: it was simplistically defined as the value of the concerned imports multiplied by tariff changes a definition that allows across-the-board calculations. The relative transparency and simplicity of the instruments used also allowed the technique of tariff bindings to be used as an effective commitment device: "nullification and impairment" tactics by countries seeking to reimpose protection through the back door are difficult to hide, as they will generally fall foul of the GATT national treatment rule and the prohibition on quotas (Article XI). Without the constraint of tariff bindings many of the GATT disciplines become unenforceable.

These two conditions are not fulfilled in the services context. Tariffs on services are rare. Non tariff barriers in services are difficult to translate into tariff equivalents, if only because governments are not always aware of their existence (regulations inhibiting trade in services often were introduced so long ago that it becomes difficult to recognize their effects as an impediment). This issue is serious because services are much more regulation intensive than goods (and often good reasons exist for such regulations) and because the economic linkages and interdependencies between services and between services and goods sectors (the input-output coefficients in national accounts) are less well understood than those that prevail between goods. Policymakers are more cognizant of the importance of steel for auto production than they are of efficient insurance or marketing services. As commitment mechanisms in the GATS are inherently weaker than in the GATT, the ultimate consequence is that it is much easier for a government to find a way to undo (deliberately or unintentionally) what has been agreed to in a GATS negotiation in other words, nullification and impairment will be more difficult to prove.

This situation has an important implication: trade and investment liberalization in services will inevitably be less susceptible to the reciprocal, market access dynamics that drive WTO negotiations. Governments must supply a large dose of "unilateralism" if they are to achieve the goal of uniform protection. Paradoxically, this necessity may be a smaller burden for developing countries than for industrial WTO members. In the past twenty years, trade liberalization in goods by developing countries has largely been the result of unilateral measures. What the developing countries did in the Tokyo and Uruguay Rounds was mostly limited to the partial binding of these unilateral reforms they did not actively engage in the GATT game. As a result, for most of the developing countries, the coming years of negotiations in services will have an "air de deja vu." The high dose of unilateralism required for liberalizing services will be supported by the recognition of the high costs of granting services high rates of protection against foreign competition (and often domestic as well).

Current levels of services protection are as high if not higher than those applied to goods ten or fifteen years ago. In many instances, the available information on the level of protection suggests average ad valorem tariff equivalents ranging from 50 percent to 100 percent for large sectors clearly more than rates observable for manufactured goods in OECD countries, but similar to the rates existing in developing countries in the early 1980s. Some analysts estimate that the U.S. Jones Act (which restricts maritime cabotage to U.S. flag vessels) increases prices by 100 to 300 percent over the average world price. The effects of similar restrictions in developing countries are analogous. Fees charged by the (monopoly) public companies providing port services for handling and storage of goods in Egypt are some 30 percent higher than in neighboring countries. Adopting a more competitive regulatory regime for telecommunications in Egypt has been estimated to generate a net welfare gain of $800 million, or 1.2 percent of GDP.

The need for unilateral action to undertake the reforms required to attain neutrality has implications for the process of formulating negotiating positions in multilateral (or regional) forums and determining who should take the lead in negotiations on services. In sharp contrast with trade in goods, services liberalization efforts must rely much more firmly on central decision makers as opposed to the negotiating process if these efforts are to be an effective tool for economic development. In liberalization of trade in goods, mercantilist trade negotiators could play a central role with only limited potential to do significant economic harm to the national economy the principal harm done derived from the opportunity costs of not pursuing deeper (unilateral) reforms, something that presumably was not a feasible option for many GATT members because of domestic political constraints; and the non uniformity that inherently emerges from "offer-request" type negotiations. The main reasons for the beneficial outcome were that the mechanics of reciprocity were needed to overcome resistance to liberalization, and that trade barriers (tariffs or non tariff trade barriers) were prevalent enough and of a type that allowed the process to work. Trade negotiators had an obvious focal point (the level of trade barriers) and could go about their business, "doing good" in the process. This dynamic is less likely to prevail in services. Reciprocity can play less of a role because exporters play a smaller role, and non border protection is dominant. The former implies that in many developing countries opposition to reform and liberalization cannot be counterbalanced by export interests seeking better access to foreign service markets; the latter implies that trade negotiators do not have equivalent focal points and the necessary information to employ the tools of their trade in a manner that guarantees the outcome is welfare improving. At issue in the services context are generally regulatory regimes that cannot (should not) be altered in incremental ways. In contrast to tariffs that can be changed smoothly and continuously, regulatory regimes are often "lumpy" any change will generally be discrete and not necessarily in the national interest. In short, the onus will be on autonomous, national reform that must be undertaken and led by central decision makers.

From this perspective, contrary to what is often said, developing countries may not need to expand greatly the capacities of their trade negotiators to "negotiate." Instead, the focus of attention should be on strengthening and maintaining a robust capacity for identifying, understanding, and designing the domestic regulatory reforms that need to be undertaken in services in order to enhance the efficiency of the economy and bolster economic growth prospects. Multilateral negotiations and institutions should be seen and used as a facilitating device to support the process of implementing the reforms, not as the driver of reform.

Implementing the Uniformity Principle

Regulatory reforms in services should aim, directly or indirectly, at the establishment of a more uniform system of intervention. Attaining this objective will involve deregulation elimination of outdated, hence costly and inefficient, regulations, including restrictions on foreign entry and re-regulation the adoption of appropriate, market- (efficiency-) enhancing regulations. Although services liberalization does not raise new conceptual issues, it does raise new technical issues. Being less tradable than goods, services are more directly dependent on factor markets in the country of consumption the market for labor, land, and specific bundles of factors often described in certain network services under the generic name of "essential facilities." In the case of goods, a specific (non uniform) treatment of factors of production can be circumvented by firms by moving production to the cheapest available location: specificity in the policy stance toward factors does not hurt foreign competitors, nor domestic consumers, as long as protection is uniform. As the degrees of freedom for choosing the location of production are more limited in services, the costs of specific policies toward essential facilities can be higher. This point is well known in relationship to barriers to access to essential facilities in telecoms.

However, it is not limited to network services such as telecoms, energy, railways, or air transport. For instance, essential facilities in retailing may consist of a piece of well-located real estate and associated transport infrastructures that are well designed to attract shoppers: restrictions on large shops (or even mere zoning regulations on the authorized type of buildings for different areas) could then constitute a serious barrier to potential entrants because they create an artificial scarcity of usable land or infrastructures.

Thus services liberalization requires a strong focus on attaining and maintaining uniform non border protection. The domestic reform agenda is frequently complex, with progress being hampered by resistance by vested interests. Entry barriers often create significant rents for incumbents, who have a strong interest in blocking attempts by governments to increase the contestability of "their" markets. The primary need is to ensure that potential entrants are free to enter service markets and that policies do not discriminate against foreign as opposed to domestic entrants. Entry barriers in many service activities tend to be justified by invoking market failure rationales that revolve around information asymmetries, fears of excessive entry, the need for universal service, and so on. While there is often a valid rationale for intervention (regulation), this does not generally require the creation of significant legal entry barriers.

In the case of developing countries, pursuit of a domestic reform agenda may be easier to pursue because some of the aspects of regulatory reforms that are important in industrial countries are less prevalent. For example, the number and political strength of domestic service industries are often smaller than in industrialized countries as there tends to be excess demand for efficient services. Moreover, "sunk" costs (costs generated by components of an infrastructure that have few if any alternative uses) are likely to be small in many least-developed countries because past investments have been small or have not been maintained (as illustrated by the situation of many public telecom companies in least-developed countries). Moreover, sunk cost bottlenecks related to network infrastructures may be slow to emerge in developing countries if central decision makers make choices in terms of service-led competition, rather than infrastructure based competition. For many developing countries, what is needed are well-functioning services consistent with the prevailing scarcity of capital so as to minimize the cost of needed infrastructure.

This reasoning can be applied, mutatis mutandis, to non network services as well. For instance, in many least-developed countries, many of the state-owned ships that were purchased in a wave of implementation of the UNCTAD liner conference codes have little value, except as a source of scrap iron. In some countries state-owned shipping companies often consist of a small management team, which grants operating licenses under the costly (collusive) rules of the UNCTAD codes and eventually (but not always) derives rents from this situation. Here again sunk costs are less of a constraint than in OECD countries.

Another possible difference between regulatory reforms in developing and industrial countries concerns the trade-off between equity and efficiency. In industrial countries, regulatory reforms can be detrimental to certain groups of consumers or citizens. This possibility seems more remote in developing countries (particularly in the least-developed countries) because most of the existing service monopolies are currently far from providing universal service of uniform good quality (telecoms, airlines, roads, and so on). In other words, the concerns about "universal service" in certain industrial countries (with their strong protectionist potential) may be less important in many developing countries, simply because this objective has not (yet) been attained.

Because there is less scope for international outsourcing (geographic "splintering" of production), the political economy of services liberalization should be easier than it is for goods. Labor is less likely to be put into a situation where whole industries are confronted with a high probability of total demise because the country is unable to produce the goods concerned efficiently. Instead, new entrants will need to employ local labor and produce services locally. Users of services which include manufacturing firms are more likely to be sensitive to the argument that inefficient service industries cannot be tolerated because many services are vital determinants of their ability to compete on world markets.

Determining Priorities and Designing Domestic Reforms

Regulatory reform is a complex process, especially if the objective of uniformity is taken seriously. Nonetheless, both economic theory and cross-country experience suggest a number of steps that can be taken by governments in determining the need for and the design of policy reforms.

First, regulatory reforms require a proper definition of the "relevant markets" that are affected or involved. Although in principle a general equilibrium approach is required in the assessment of policies all activities have to be put "on a par" in practice this is impossible to put into operation. Instead, efforts should be made to identify the appropriate nexus of related, interdependent activities. For instance, liberalizing air transport without liberalizing airport slots does not lead very far: the price of air tickets will mirror both competitive pressures in terms of routes (if there are several airlines in presence, which is not necessarily the case) and monopoly rents related to airport slot monopolies. Another example is maritime transport Joe Francois and Ian Wooton estimate that the welfare gains from trade liberalization (better access to markets) may be doubled if complementary actions are taken to increase competition in the shipping sector. Yet another example is cross-subsidization between network services, such as between telecom and electricity (a electricity monopolist could cross-subsidize its telecom activities, in particular if the technology is developed to use electricity cables to send telecom signals). A "general" general-equilibrium framework is too complicated to be conceived and managed by decision makers. Thus "partial" general-equilibrium frameworks should be developed, each of which constitutes a cluster of interrelated services activities. This pragmatic approach could be based on the well-known "effective rate of assistance" (ERA) concept.

Such an approach could build on two tracks. First, a government could estimate ERAs based on all taxes and subsidies that apply to a broadly defined service activity (such as audiovisuals, tourism, telecoms, and so on), the major inputs into this activity (goods and services), and the factors of production used. Input-output tables and social accounting matrices are a vital tool in determining the various clusters of activities and their major inputs. This "public budget-based" component of the ERA can be complemented by a "private" sector component where businesses producing the services involved would be invited to identify the border and non border policies that they perceive to be crucial impediments to their ability to contest markets (at home and abroad), and to provide qualitative (quantitative, if they exist) information on these elements. For example, the ERA for tourism in a Sub-Saharan African country could take into account the explicit taxes and subsidies on hotels, wildlife parks, telecoms, airport slots and airlines, as well as the impediments, more difficult to measure, that limit the country's capacity to attract, ship, and host foreign visitors to and between its major tourism sites. It is important to underline that the goal of such an exercise is not to favor any particular activity but rather to ensure that all the services under examination are roughly treated the same way in terms of explicit support (or taxation).

Clearly such an exercise will be information- and resource-intensive and require substantial analytical input. The institution that is given the task of undertaking the required analysis should have the ability to collect, compile, and process a wide range of quantitative and qualitative information. The type of institution that is required is one that has been termed a transparency or competition-advocacy body in the literature. The Australian Productivity Commission is a good example. In a number of economies in transition this role has been played to some extent by the Competition Office. Many governments may find it difficult to establish and staff such an institution, and many may not be able to devote adequate resources for its operation. However, almost all countries have access to competent officials, legal experts, and academics. What is required is a policy decision to establish the required institution, provide it with the necessary mandate to undertake the work required, and, most importantly, to consider seriously the results of its work.

Given information on the ERAs across clusters, a number of simple rules of thumb for regulatory reforms can be identified. First, such efforts in services should aim at reducing the highest ERAs first. Besides directly targeting policies that give rise to high ERAs, efforts should center on increasing the level of competition in markets. Competition is the engine for providing the benefits expected from regulatory reform. This requires the abolition of legislated and administrative barriers to entry in sectors where there is no compelling economic rationale for maintaining such barriers. To maximize the benefits of such initiatives, no distinction should be made between domestic (national) and foreign firms as benefits from increasing access to markets are generally maximized if foreign firms are able to contest markets. A lesson from the experience of OECD countries in this connection is not to rely too much on the ability of competition law and rulings to deliver a high level of competitive pressure in services. For instance, there is an emerging recognition that competition cases in the telecoms area have led to stalemate situations, rather than enhancing competition. When initiating domestic regulatory reforms, developing countries should consider adopting direct mechanisms to deliver a prompt increase in competitive pressures. For instance, Guatemala has introduced a dispute settlement mechanism based on "final offer arbitration" (administered by a specific industry regulator), and this method seems to have delivered more rapid gains from service liberalization than competition law court-based disputes. A growing literature provides rules of thumb or criteria to identify whether an "acceptable" level of competition exists in a given service industry at a given period. For instance, air routes with fewer than three operating airlines are unlikely to be under intensive competition, and large gains from regulatory reforms can be expected. In the case of multimodal competition (such as between trains and airlines), price comparisons between similar air routes with and without multimodal competition can be a good proxy for assessing the capacity of regulatory reforms to deliver the benefits of increased competition.

Both the OECD and emerging market experience illustrate the need to consider strengthening regulatory supervision for some sectors where asymmetric information and related problems prevail regulatory reform can entail re-regulation as well as de-regulation. The OECD experience also underlines the need to enhance the ability of governments to generate and have access to a wide body of accurate information to allow an assessment of the impact of policy changes and to identify priorities for reform. Where regulation is called for, this is best done by ad hoc specialized agencies. However, such institutions will give rise to high risks of non uniform protection and are also open to capture by vested interests. Another rule of thumb is therefore that regulatory agencies, and more generally the government broadly defined, be subjected to the scrutiny of the "apex" transparency institution mentioned earlier that has the mandate to assess the economic impact of their activities and is responsible for providing recommendations to assist government in the pursuit of neutrality of policy.

The importance of strengthening capacity to collect and analyze information cannot be overemphasized. A common mistake made by governments involved in regulatory reform is to reduce the ability of agencies to compile the information needed to monitor the impact of reforms. Relatively good information on prices prevailing in liberalized services can be obtained rapidly and cheaply, as illustrated by telecoms or energy. These encouraging developments suggest that the absence of information in services may be more a consequence of old regulations and market closure than an intrinsic feature of service industries. It also suggests that the ERA approach could be more useful than might be expected today for estimating ad valorem tariff equivalents of regulatory barriers.

GATS Negotiations to the Domestic Reform Agenda

The reliance on unilateral, autonomous initiative that is required to pursue a growth-enhancing domestic regulatory reform agenda and increase competition on service markets does not eliminate the benefits from multilateral cooperation. A multilateral liberalization effort can be beneficial in moving the world closer to the ideal of free trade by helping to remove regulatory barriers to entry in service industries and increasing the global information base on the level and impact of these barriers.

In some countries, vested interests are powerful enough to block welfare-improving reforms. In such cases, multilateral negotiations offer an opportunity to break the political deadlock. This of course is a basic rationale for reciprocity in WTO negotiations as long as the agenda includes enough items that can help change the domestic political equilibrium, it can support beneficial reforms. However, as discussed, the relevance of this argument is likely to be limited for many developing countries. In the case of services, in the early stages of liberalization, little support for reform can be expected to emerge from (potential) exporters of services. In general, in most countries there are unlikely to be many (potentially) competitive exporters of services, if any. When there is a political economy rationale for pursuing reforms through a multilateral mechanism, issue linkages will be required to areas outside services, as that is where developing countries have the greatest export interests examples include disciplining the use of contingent protection and reducing barriers to trade in agricultural products.

At the same time, the opposition of domestic firms to the prospect of increased pressure from imports may not be as strong in services as in goods, especially if there are scale or scope economies. Indeed, those that liberalize first may have a strategic advantage a point underlined by economic analysis and present in the minds of many service providers who are more eager to liberalize, even in the absence of narrow reciprocity, that is, "equivalent" concessions being offered by trading partners. This suggests care should be taken not to fall into a "negotiation trap" seeking to apply standard GATT techniques of regarding liberalization commitments as "concessions" for which compensation must be obtained. What is required is the pursuit of the national reform agenda. The approach should be akin to a more or less explicit joint or concerted exercise in unilateral liberalization. Any "concessions" to be negotiated should center on the time frame for reaching a common threshold of liberalization or the implementation of an agreement that is required to develop and strengthen the institutions needed to implement a particular reform that is deemed welfare enhancing. Conversely, all proposals that are not welfare enhancing should be rejected.

Although this approach may sound idealistic and unrealistic, it is a good description of the European Communities (EC's) Single Market exercise in services. Perhaps the best illustration is the recent electricity case, where some member states did not hesitate to liberalize much more quickly and deeply than others, underlining the nonreciprocal approach. Similar dynamics arose in the WTO negotiations on financial services and telecoms. The success of these sectoral talks largely reflected the fact that most of the governments involved were convinced of the need to pursue regulatory reforms in these sectors, including liberalization and elimination of entry barriers. This was a precondition for the agreements to materialize it was clear that the associated regulatory reforms did not go beyond what had already been accomplished or decided in the national (unilateral) context.

To be able to participate effectively and maximize the benefits of GATS negotiations it is vital that governments come prepared, that is, develop a well-defined domestic reform agenda they desire to pursue. Only countries that have already identified their domestic regulatory reform agenda can arrive at the negotiating table with an adequate sense of what proposals are in their interest and the ability to reap the benefits from the exchange of information that occurs during negotiations. A country having no or little information on its own services-sector-related policies and without a clear domestic strategy will be flying blind in GATS discussions. As mentioned, this is less of a problem in merchandise trade talks because a country always has information on its own tariffs and related trade policies, and in any event, the policies that are on the table are generally policies that it would be desirable to eliminate. This is not the case with services, which points again to the need to come prepared with a clear domestic reform agenda that aims to attain a more uniform pattern of protection (that is, neutrality). Economically meaningful choices regarding the design and sequencing of regulatory reforms aimed at increasing competition in domestic service markets require a profound knowledge about effective resource allocation and ERAs in the economy that trade negotiators do not have. Central decision makers must therefore not only design and pursue a national reform strategy but provide clear instructions and briefs to their officials who represent them in negotiations.

A major beneficial role that can be played by GATS/ WTO is to assist member governments attain and maintain a neutral economy-wide sectoral policy stance. This can be done through design of the disciplines (rules) that are negotiated and enforced and through the creation of mechanisms that foster transparency and generate information. A first and minimum requirement is that GATS covers all services. There is no rationale for excluding certain sectors or modes of supply from the national treatment and market access disciplines of GATS. Given that GATS allows for derogations to both principles, at the very least comprehensive scheduling will ensure that a government is forced to consider the justification and economic rationale for the policies it maintains that are not in conformity with these principles. One way of moving toward this is to apply a formula approach to expanded coverage in the next round of negotiations, setting minimum coverage targets for GATS members, to be attained by a specified date (which may vary depending on per capita income level to allow for a transition period). A more ambitious approach would be to seek agreement on a deadline for full coverage to be reached. It seems unlikely that WTO members will be willing to consider moving from a positive to a negative list approach to scheduling commitments but there is nothing to prevent individual countries from doing so. Whatever formula or focal point is established for the negotiations, individual countries should consider going beyond this. In the process valuable information can be obtained on how different policies affect clusters of activities that are interrelated and interdependent.

Second, the focus of attention should be on identifying what horizontal, cross-sectoral disciplines can contribute to the realization of the principle of uniform protection. In the GATS context this implies that scheduling of liberalization commitments should shift from the sectoral (specific) to the horizontal (general). Ideally, given universal scheduling of services sectors by a country, restrictions should be of a horizontal (across the-board) nature, and negotiating efforts should center on developing disciplines that make sense from the perspective of long-term growth and economic development. In general, these are likely to focus on safeguarding the contestability of markets while maintaining national sovereignty to regulate activities to attain health, safety, prudential, and related objectives. In this perspective, it would be useful to consider "generalizing" the appropriate parts of the so-called Reference Paper in telecoms in order to make it a "horizontal" set of disciplines to be included into GATS as such. The Reference Paper includes concepts such as "affecting the terms of participation" and "essential facilities" that could usefully be extended to all services, even those without any background of monopoly or public ownership or control.

Third, a strict policy of most favored nation treatment is desirable. The appropriate geographical scope of regulatory reforms depends on the extent to which decisions by national authorities do not internalize external effects across jurisdictions. In this context, regional liberalization of transactions in services can provide a positive economic outcome, in contrast to the case of trade in merchandise where there is more cause for concern about trade diversion. However, to the extent that regulatory reforms pursued in the regional context can be applied on a nondiscriminatory basis which the available evidence suggests is generally the case there is less need to worry about the discriminatory effects of regional cooperation. On all these dimensions identifying prevailing policies and their effects on clusters of activities, assessing modalities of disciplines that seek to increase the contestability of service markets, and determining whether (how) regulatory reforms are (can be) applied on a nondiscriminatory basis a multilateral institution such as the WTO can play a very constructive role in assisting governments to implement and maintain a coherent development strategy. Designing a regulatory reform program to achieve greater uniformity in incentives is difficult. Multilateral surveillance of domestic policies can help in monitoring the prevailing policy stance and identifying areas where action may be required. Moreover, multilateral cooperation is required to reduce the competition-reducing effect of domestic regulations, especially in mandatory standards for product safety, professional certification, prudential regulation, and so on. This is perhaps the major area where future efforts should focus, not least because it is one where unilateral action is inherently limited.

Summary

This chapter has sought to identify a number of rules of thumb for decision makers in developing countries in the run-up toward the next round of multilateral negotiations to be launched in 2000. The characteristics of services markets have several implications for the process of multilateral negotiations.

First and foremost, decision makers should seek to adopt a policy stance that reduces the existing dispersion in the level of support or assistance that is given to activities. Uniformity of protection should be the primary rule of thumb. This in turn requires that information be collected and compiled to allow decision makers to identify priorities and the indirect effects of existing regulatory interventions across sectors and activities.

Second, governments cannot rely on the familiar process of reciprocal exchange of "concessions." Instead, a pro-active policy stance is required that is firmly centered on a domestic reform agenda. Much of what is required to ensure that the WTO process is a facilitator of the adoption of policies that will support economic development will have to be undertaken unilaterally. Developing countries can expect very little from playing the traditional reciprocity game that has been pursued by OECD countries to good effect in liberalizing their merchandise trade. In many cases, developing countries' informational deficit will be bigger, their service export interests less powerful, and their import-related interests more friendly to liberalization a modern development strategy requires cheap and abundant differentiated intermediate services, and the sunk-cost-motivated resistance to liberalization that is observed in OECD countries is less likely to prevail.

Many observers have noted that GATS is an imperfect instrument. Notwithstanding the deficiencies, it can be used as a commitment and signaling device by governments that have decided that regulatory reforms are in the national interest. Specific commitments can be made for all modes of supply, including FDI, and governments that have decided to open access to services markets to foreign providers should pursue the option of locking in policy reforms as much as possible through the existing GATS mechanisms. Future efforts to expand GATS disciplines should center on expanding the sectoral coverage of the agreement and strengthening the transparency and information collection and dissemination functions of the WTO Secretariat.

4

Globalisation, Democracy and Trade Policy

Introduction

It has not only become the focus of serious research and discussion among academics, business people, bureaucrats and politicians but has also become the focus of almost daily discussions among people of different spheres of society. There is a vast literature on the subject, and almost anybody has a very strong opinion about what globalisation means and what kind of changes it will bring about. As one would expect, academics cannot agree on globalisation either. For one school of thought it is nothing new, but for another and it would seem that this one is supported by the majority globalisation is a 'completely new ball game'. Globalisation is seen as a new engine for producing prosperity and higher income in many countries. But it is creating a new problem concerning income distribution both within and between countries in that it will create 'winners and losers'. It is very well known that losers will fight to stop the process that makes them losers, whereas winners will take what they can get without actively supporting globalisation. This is the fundamental challenge for democracies. Furthermore, because trade policy is seen as a major tool for pushing globalisation, groups in societies and countries opposing globalisation are also resisting a further liberalisation of world trade. Instead, these groups are demanding a democratisation of trade policies as well as a democratic WTO as the major 'agent' of free trade. In this chapter, I will focus my discussion on three questions:

- the challenge of globalisation for democracy;
- the challenges of globalisation and the demand for a 'democratic trade policy' for international organisations like the WTO; and
- scenarios and policy options for governments to respond to the challenge of globalisation.

Globalisation and 'localisation': Challenge for democracy

The process of globalisation is a profound challenge for democracies, since it is eroding national boundaries, weakening the authority of the state and could undermine the support of the people for democratically elected governments, at least in principle. In a globalised economy, the scale of economic activity no longer corresponds to the territory of the nation-state but is global and transnational. The whole purpose of a democratic system is to make sure that power is shifted back to the people and not left with a small elite. Therefore, the democratic principle of free elections is a very important one.

However, democracy does not necessarily involve the direct participation of the citizens in the political decision-making process. Instead, Western democratic political systems accept the principle of democratic representation and responsibility. This principle underlies the transfer of power to the winners of elections for the specific period of time for which they have been elected. As a result of that process, a competition between political elites takes place over political positions and political values.

All democratic political systems are linked to a region, a society, a state and maybe a nation-state. Democratic governments of those nation-states are elected by the people to govern the state, to protect the people and implement policies that are in the interests of the people and are supported by the people. In a globalised world, however, societies and states are more and more influenced from the outside, and governments cannot stop this negative influence.

This raises profound questions for all democratic political systems. First, if democracy is linked to the nation-state but the governments of those states are no longer powerful enough to control and manage influence from outside, could those developments lead to the 'death of democracy'? Second, if national democratic political systems are no longer the controlling force, what kind of democratic institutions outside the state could take on this responsibility? Third, if national democratic systems are becoming weaker, does it make sense to work towards a global democratic system, a democratic world government?

Globalisation and Democracy

In today's world there are more liberal democratic countries than ever before. Especially in the 1980s and even more so after the end of the Cold War in the 1990s, more and more countries moved from an undemocratic to a democratic political system. But in the light of profound challenges for all democracies, some observers are afraid that the best days of democracy may already be behind us. Arthur Schlesinger, for example, argued that in the face of globalisation and the erosion of the traditional nation-state, the twenty-first century might see a decline in liberal democracy rather than a further step ahead.

Second, is the nation-state still in the driver's seat? In the global economy, new boundaries are being drawn between countries, business and international institutions. As the saying goes: most nation-states are too big for the small problems and at the same time are too small for the big problems. Jessica Mathews put it succinctly:

Increasingly, resources and threats that matter, including money, information, pollution and popular culture, circulate and shape lives and economies with little regard for political boundaries. Even the most powerful states find the marketplace and international public opinion compelling them more often to follow a particular course.

Indeed, governments no longer have a monopoly on power-other powerful institutions are emerging. Governments are therefore less able to control, dominate and manage events, but they face more complex problems. Just to mention a few of the challenges to national governments posed by a globalising world: a global financial and economic crisis will lead to economic problems and to a decline in living standards. These problems cannot be solved by any national government, but at the same time, national governments will be held responsible by their electorates for the problems. And national governments are no more able to cope alone with environmental problems, drug trafficking, migration problems, nuclear issues, energy problems, regional wars, and so on. In fighting all these problems, more and more countries are realising that it is better to cooperate.

But the requirement for cooperation between countries is that the nation-states are still in control and that they are still powerful enough to work together efficiently to solve problems. All of that changes with globalisation. The natural boundaries of states are being eroded, and globalisation is creating new boundaries, most of the time not linked to the nation-state. Globalisation leads to global markets with global players, but there is no powerful referee on this global level to make sure that a level playing field is created and that the global players are playing a 'fair game'. The forces behind globalisation have uprooted the old boundaries of the nation-state. In today's world, those forces are first of all technology and telecommunications.

'Localisation' and Democracy

There is a dilemma: on the one hand, the process of globalisation that is going on is weakening nation-states and with it governments' ability to care for national interests and to protect national sovereignty; on the other hand, in many democracies a process is going on that can be called 'localisation', which means that more and more people become involved in the political decision-making process on a local level. In terms of strengthening a democratic political system, this means more direct participation of citizens and as a result a more active democracy.

There is a strong incentive for politicians to listen to the people because politicians are elected and re-elected on a local level. As famous House Speaker Tip O'Neill put it: 'All politics is local'. If politicians do not listen to the people, some groups will join hands and work together as non-governmental organisations (NGOs) or street opposition or single-issue coalitions. We saw many of those groups demonstrating in Seattle in December 1999 opposing further liberalisation of world trade.

NGOs focus on special issues that are supported by people in society who think that they are not represented by politicians and political parties and that they are not heard in the political decision-making process. And the evidence so far is that those groups will grow stronger in democracies because of globalisation. The economic process of globalisation will lead to higher income and a better living standard on a global level. But this higher income is linked to the problem of how to distribute this new wealth how to distribute it between countries and how to distribute it within societies. The losers in globalisation will naturally oppose it, and that will create a backlash against globalisation at a local level. And because politicians are elected at a local level, those groups can become more powerful in a democratic political system. The winners in globalisation will, first of all, quite often not know if and when they will be winners- and if they do know, they will take it for granted and will not work actively to support globalisation.

How to adapt democratic systems?

Globalisation in that sense poses two profound challenges to democracy. First, globalisation threatens democracy as such because democratic political systems are based on the territorial state and this state is being eroded by the process of globalisation. Second, globalisation poses a threat to the democratic political system because globalisation will lead to a profound restructuring process on a global level that will create many losers at a local level. It will create a political resistance against globalisation and possibly a challenge for the democratic systems at a national level. Both developments will result in a loss of democracy.

To respond to these problems it will be necessary to work towards strengthening the democratic political system, for example by implementing measures to strengthen parliaments and to obtain domestic support first before adapting to new global structures. Also, governments could decide to opt out if they cannot obtain the necessary domestic support. Furthermore, NGOs could become a new element of democratic control, assuming that NGOs could get the authority for such a role in a democratic political system.

However, the basic question remains: how could democracies, which depend on the territorial state, cope with the global challenges posed by globalisation? The straightforward answer would be that globalisation requires a world government, but in reality, democracies will have to cope with the challenges of globalisation without a world government for the time being. But one could think about how to adapt the political systems and how democracy should be changed to respond to globalisation.

David Held thinks it could be done, and he argues in favour of a cosmopolitan democracy. One element of that approach would be to change the territorial boundaries of responsibility to make sure that areas like international financial markets, which are currently outside of any democratic control, are brought into a broadly defined democratic political system.

Second, regional and global institutions should be reformed to make them a more acceptable part of the political process. Third, a new international democratic process should include groups that so far are outside the decision-making process. However, this is just the beginning of a process that might lead in the long term towards a global government and a world parliament. As an alternative with a medium-term perspective, Wolfgang Reinicke proposes a global public policy, not a world government but a mixed approach to global management in which states, corporations, NGOs, regional and international organisations, and coalitions cooperate. Such a new approach would have the potential to improve the capacities of governments and international organisations to cope with the challenges of globalisation and its effects.

Need of democratic WTO

The WTO is criticised for being an undemocratic international organisation lacking transparency and deciding behind closed doors as a 'rich man's club' without broad participation. Many of these critics of the WTO demonstrated in Seattle and made it a lively event. However, important members of the WTO are responsible for the disaster in Seattle as well. The problem is very well known and is a profound one: should international organisations like the WTO become democratic institutions, or should the WTO just play the role of an agency implementing the policies and rules that are decided by the WTO member states?

John Jackson is one of the best-known experts on the evolution of world trade law and the WTO as an organisation. Concerning the criticism voiced against the WTO, he put it succinctly:

Clearly, the WTO is not a 'perfect' institution. It still represents some of the older ideas of conducting 'diplomacy', which called for secrecy and elitism. Observers are critical of the WTO 's lack of transparency, the lack of opportunities for broad participation by various private citizen groups and NGOs, and the (sometimes) seeming lack of 'democratic legitimacy' for some of its decisions. The WTO will have to reconcile the need for international co-operative action with a respect for the constraints placed on its capacity for action.

Does globalisation demand a democratic trade policy and a democratic WTO? Globalisation creates two problems of democratic legitimacy, one on a national level and the other on an international level. On a national level, we are talking about different political systems. All twenty-nine OECD countries are democracies, and all are members of the WTO. But there are currently 135 WTO members, about half of which are considered democratic states. In democracies, the trade policy decision-making process is per se a democratic one. In a democracy, all groups are invited to participate in the political process. In the end, of course, the majority will decide.

If is therefore quite likely that small groups will take part in the decision-making process but will not be successful. These groups can respond in one of three ways in trying to become a more powerful force in the democratic decision-making process. First, they can try to obtain the support of more people in a society to become a more powerful group. Second, they can work together with other groups to build a coalition focusing on specific issues. Third, they can stay as a small group but nevertheless become a powerful force in the political process by playing the 'political game' more efficiently than others.

Several of these small but powerful groups are well organised, focus on specific issues and are well connected politically in such a way that they can play a much more important role in the political process than one would expect from looking at the size of the group.

The agricultural lobby in many countries is a good example of that kind of powerful and efficient small group in a democratic political system.

Democratic member states or a democratic WTO

The second problem of democratic legitimacy is the question of how to democratise international organisations like the WTO, assuming that this should be done. We are not talking about international organisations with democratic countries as members. Taking this criterion, in most international organisations democratic countries are in the minority. That is true of the WTO, UNCTAD, the World Bank and the IMF. As I have mentioned, all OECD members are democratic countries, and all these organisations were founded for a specific purpose and are controlled by the member states. These international organisations are not considered as an element of a democratic global government. They are much more special agencies with specific agendas that are set by the member states, and they are controlled by their member states.

Clearly, criticising the WTO as an undemocratic institution is meant to focus on critical democratic deficiencies, on the lack of transparency, on the lack of accountability, and on insufficient mechanisms for popular participation. This last point has been a source of strong criticism of the WTO, particularly by environmental groups, which argue that NGOs can bring important expertise and information to bear on WTO questions. Ever more NGOs are arguing along these lines. So far, however, there seem to be no explicit general rules regarding a role for NGOs in the various WTO activities. The WTO language speaks of 'appropriate arrangements'. At a minimum, there seems to be room for improvement to provide some role for NGOs within the WTO. However, the problem is the lack of democratic legitimacy of NGOs. NGOs are not democratically elected representatives of a society. They represent special interest groups.

Democratising the WTO therefore raises the question of creating a WTO parliament with elected members from the member states. Rubens Ricupero, secretary-general of UNCTAD, in a public lecture in Berlin in January 2000, called for a 'world parliament on globalisation', extending the issue of democratic deficiencies to other international organisations as well. But for the time being, a democratic world government with a world parliament of democratically elected members will not become reality. And in terms of what the WTO (and other international organisations) is supposed to do, it is questionable if in today's world a 'democratic WTO' would be desirable.

The profound challenge is the question of what is more important: efficiency or democracy? Is it better to have an efficient WTO with some democratic deficiencies, or is it more important to move towards a more democratic WTO that is most likely to be a less efficient organisation? One should keep in mind that the WTO is not a world government and is not supposed to become one. The WTO is an organisation with currently 135 member countries, all of which joined voluntarily. Another thirty countries are negotiating to become WTO members. All are interested in an efficient WTO to make sure that a 'rules-based' trade regime will work. Democratic deficiencies are, first of all, a problem of the member states. What the WTO is lacking is more a problem of transparency and opening up to citizen groups like NGOs and less a problem of creating a 'democratic WTO'

Globalisation is a challenge for all societies

Globalisation is a fact of life. However, it is a double-edged sword, a powerful new engine of the world economy that raises economic growth, spreads new technology and increases living standards in rich and poor countries alike, but also an immensely controversial process that assaults national sovereignty, erodes local culture and tradition and threatens economic, social and political instability. Globalisation weakens the territorial state because countries are no longer seen as distinct economic entities. Companies and financial markets, for example, increasingly disregard national borders when making production, marketing and investment decisions.

What is needed is a broadly based discussion in all countries and societies about the effects of globalisation and about the challenges. Especially in democratic countries, it is important to organise an ongoing debate about all aspects of globalisation, including all relevant groups and if possible the whole society. Countries could try to stay away from a globalised world to avoid the negative effects, but then they would not gain from globalisation either.

Globalisation has already brought about profound change for many societies. But we are just at the beginning of the process. Societies will have to cope with that challenge, but they are ill-prepared for it. Many people are afraid of globalisation, and there is a growing backlash against it in important countries. What is needed is a basic understanding by the people of what globalisation is all about, what kind of positive and negative effects it will bring and how citizens and groups in societies will be affected and can respond to it. Creating this kind of understanding in a society is a difficult task that requires an ongoing process of learning how to adapt to a globalised world.

It can be done, and it has been done before. Important elements are market economies, open markets, free trade: all of that required the same kind of learning process in the societies involved. Member states of the European Union face the same problem: it is hard work to 'educate' people that taking part in the European integration process is a worthwhile effort because many citizens are against it as long as they react emotionally and are not forced to think carefully about all aspects of European integration.

Globalisation will further democracy

The second element must be democracy. Governments should support democratic developments at home and abroad. In 1999, a broad coalition of states ranging in size from Cape Verde to India came together and proclaimed at a United Nations Commission on Human Rights session that all individuals have a right to democracy. Only Cuba and China abstained. Human rights have been accepted as universal rights for all individuals for many decades. Even so, there are still different opinions among governments about how to define and protect those rights.

The third element of a modern state is a market economy. A good example for countries that are supporting all three elements is the twenty-nine OECD countries: they share the principles of the market economy, pluralist democracy and respect for human rights. There seems to be a growing worldwide consensus that freer trade must also protect human rights, the environment and decent working conditions. This growing consensus is supported by environmentalists, consumer advocates, human rights activists and trade unions. The message of these groups in Seattle was loud and clear. However, these groups depend on a democratic environment and have to compete within a democratic political system.

Supporting countries that are moving towards a democratic political system will also create a more democratic trade policy and a more stable social and political situation in those countries. It is not true that the economic crisis in some countries and regions would undermine democratic political systems. A case in point is the Asian financial crisis of 1997, which brought down the Suharto regime that had ruled Indonesia for more than thirty years. In South Korea, Thailand and the Philippines, however, democracies survived the crisis intact.

But one has to be realistic: moving to a democratic political system in developing countries does not necessarily mean that this will automatically lead to a decentralised system with a more efficient government and better service for the people; it could also lead to more corruption. It is therefore important that those countries establishing a democratic system get the help they need. A democratic political system is a very difficult system. And the process towards more democratic countries should be supported. At the same time, one has to be aware of the problem that globalisation is posing a profound challenge to democracy and to all democratic political systems. It is therefore necessary to work towards solutions on a global level for tasks that the democratic state can no longer fulfill.

Towards a 'more democratic' trade policy

Governments should support a democratic approach to trade that must take into account the views of developing country democracies. The industrialised democracies are still the driving force, but they are no longer so powerful as to dominate all others. They need support to tackle the old and new trade challenges as well as to strengthen democratic processes within the WTO. Developing democracies should play a 'different role' in the trade decision-making process according to their volume of trade and their number and population size. The WTO is an intergovernmental organisation, and most member states do not want to create a 'democratic WTO', so the challenge is now to focus on the 'democratic deficit' of the WTO without weakening the efficient member-driven WTO.

In that respect, one could learn from other Bretton Woods institutions. For example, the International Monetary Fund (IMF) has a different decision-making process, including a smaller executive board with twenty-four executive directors, most of whom represent a group of countries. The WTO should also accept the IMF proposal to create an outside body to review the work of the organisation on a regular basis. Furthermore, the WTO could hold hearings on important issues, giving NGOs an opportunity to present and discuss their demands and proposals.

Changing the WTO, the organisation governing the trade system, in such a way would, first, improve the transparency of the WTO; second, open up the WTO system for outsiders like NGOs; and, third, would strengthen the role of developing countries in the WTO. The OECD countries should work together to move towards achieving these goals. To sum up: globalisation is indeed a profound challenge to democracy and will lead to a more democratic trade policy. This challenge will have to be dealt with on a local, regional, national and global level. On the one hand, the process of globalisation will erode the nation-state as the foundation of a democratic political system. On the other hand, enhanced participation by a broader range of players in the decision-making process on trade issues, for example, would foster consensus building. As a result, the debate about globalisation and trade issues would become more transparent and trade policy more democratic.

Governments do not really have a choice—globalisation is a fact of life and a challenge for all governments. Societies will have to cope and to adapt to a globalised world. Globalisation will lead to much tougher competition within and between countries. And if governments do not respond appropriately to the challenges of globalisation, their countries will lose in global competition and the living standards of their people could decline. Governments therefore face the task of explaining globalisation and guiding a public discussion about its effects. This will be a difficult process. However, it will lead to a more democratic trade policy and a more democratic WTO.

5

Broadening WTO Membership

Introduction

WTO membership is still less than universal. Although most developed and many developing countries are WTO members, fully one-third of the world's population, accounting for about 10 per cent of world trade and 5 per cent of world GDP, lived in countries outside the WTO system at the end of 1999.

The good news is that most of these countries (most prominently, China) have applied to join the WTO. However, while current WTO members have welcomed this move in principle, that welcome has not translated into swift and successful accession negotiations. From 1995 to 1999, only seven countries that were not previously contracting parties to GATT 1947 were admitted to the WTO (in chronological order: Ecuador, Bulgaria, Mongolia, Panama, Kyrgyzstan, Latvia and Estonia). Another thirty-three countries were at various stages of negotiating their terms of accession with current members; some, like Algeria and China, first applied to become a contracting party to GATT 1947 more than ten years ago. The thirty-three applicants are a fairly diverse group and include most CIS countries (prominently, Russia, Ukraine and Belarus), other transition economies in Asia and Europe (in addition to China, Vietnam, Laos, Cambodia and Albania), and an assortment of others, such as Chinese Taipei (Taiwan), the Gulf states, and African and Pacific island economies.

Unless accession negotiations are accelerated, many of the benefits of WTO membership will be denied to applicant countries for a prolonged period. This would be unfortunate because, particularly for the many transition economies among applicants, accession to the WTO becomes one important focus of efforts to implement market-oriented reforms in a wide range of trade-related policies. Furthermore, even if there is no full-blown Millennium Round of trade negotiations, forthcoming negotiations between current WTO members will inevitably tie up political attention and administrative capacity that would be required to complete accession negotiations with the new-comers.

Potential stumbling blocks in accession negotiations

Accession negotiations deal with two broad types of issue. First, the WTO Agreement and its annexes contain mandatory rules on the conduct of a wide range of national trade-related policies, e.g. the extension of m.f.n. treatment to WTO members, national treatment of imported goods with respect to indirect taxes, the general prohibition on quantitative import restrictions, and the protection of trade-related intellectual property rights. Accession negotiations therefore involve a detailed review of the relevant legislation and practice of applicant countries. Current members typically take the view that these must be substantially in line with WTO rules by the time an applicant joins the WTO. In recent accessions, the implementation of particular legislation was deferred until after accession in only a very few cases, with the exact timing specified in the acceding country's protocol of accession.

Accession negotiations have been protracted because, compared with GATT 1947, WTO rules are far more detailed and cover a wider range of topics, such as international trade in services (GATS) and trade-related intellectual property rights (TRIPs). Besides, many countries acceding to GATT 1947 in recent decades were developing countries that enjoyed considerable discretion in the conduct of their trade policies under Article XVIII of GATT 1947 and the amendments of 1965. Now, many candidates for accession to the

WTO are transition economies that will be subject to the full set of (extended) disciplines of the WTO Agreement.

Second, accession negotiations deal with market access for imported goods and services in applicant countries. Among GATT 1947 and WTO members, the protection offered to domestic firms has been progressively reduced as a result of successive rounds of trade negotiations; nevertheless, the level of protection still differs widely across WTO members. Relevant policy instruments include the level and dispersion of import tariffs for goods and market-access commitments in services. Accession negotiations have become protracted, inter alia because some current WTO members are using their leverage in negotiations to extract concessions from acceding countries that go much further than the commitments made by current WTO members at a similar level of economic development.

Trade in industrial goods

Acceding countries are required to bind their import tariffs, i.e. to commit themselves to not setting tariffs above specified levels. Typically, they also commit themselves to reducing bound tariff levels over an implementation period, usually of seven years from their accession to the WTO. Negotiations between applicants and incumbent members focus on the import-weighted average tariff level, the dispersion of tariff rates across products, the number of zero-rated products and the number of tariff lines for which rates are not to be bound (normally very few).

The key demand by current WTO members has been that the major acceding economies (including China and Russia) bind their tariffs for industrial goods at roughly double the average rate for OECD countries. This would imply an import-weighted average of bound rates of no more than 10 per cent. Among countries that recently joined the WTO, the simple average of individual tariff bindings was between 7 and 13 per cent for Estonia, Kyrgyzstan, Latvia, Panama and Bulgaria, and approximately 20 per cent for Ecuador and Mongolia.

By contrast, developing country WTO members still impose higher tariffs, even after implementing the Uruguay Round liberalisation. Finger estimate the post-Uruguay Round trade-weighted applied average tariff on industrial goods for twenty-six developing countries at 13 per cent; the corresponding average bound rate is 20 per cent. Furthermore, in many of these countries, tariff bindings for industrial products are not nearly comprehensive, whereas recently acceded countries as well as applicants are strongly expected to bind all tariffs.

While it can be argued that current members are applying double standards in making far-reaching demands on applicants, a more benign view would focus on the implications of their position for the evolution of the world trading system. In the Uruguay Round and successive negotiations, tariffs on industrial goods have been cut and even eliminated for some groups of products (e.g. information technology). Tariff bindings were made far more comprehensive even by developing countries, which in the past had frequently either not bound tariffs at all or had bound them at far higher levels than were actually applied. Thus, in this benign view, current WTO members are requiring applicants to be at the forefront of global tariff liberalisation rather than possibly entering the WTO with a protectionist agenda that would create obstacles in the way of further liberalisation.

Agriculture

The WTO Agreement on Agriculture has brought that sector back into the discipline of the multilateral trading system. Essentially, members' commitments under the agreement are in three broad areas. First, quantitative import restrictions are to be replaced by tariffs that are bound and subsequently reduced. Second, domestic production subsidies that strongly impact upon trade ('yellow' subsidies) are to be bound and reduced over time. Certain other production subsidies that are regarded as not affecting trade ('green' subsidies) are not restricted, while yet another category ('blue subsidies') consists of measures that have been exempted only temporarily from reduction requirements. Third, export subsidies, while not outlawed as for industrial goods (Agreement on Subsidies and Countervailing Measures), are also to be bound and reduced.

Here, the Cairns Group of countries (mainly exporters of temperate-zone agricultural products, prominently including Australia) have gone further in committing themselves to the abolition of agricultural export subsidies.

With respect to the tariffication of quantitative restrictions, applicant countries are in practice free to abolish these and propose 'target bindings' for their tariffs on agricultural imports that need not be based on an exact calculation of the tariff equivalent of the quantitative restrictions. This procedure avoids the difficulties that most applicant countries would face in quantifying the effects of policy instruments based on weak data in the context of a rapidly evolving systemic transformation.

On domestic support, the binding of production subsidies entails the calculation of the aggregate measurement of support for each basic agricultural commodity in accordance with Annex 3 of the WTO Agreement on Agriculture. This raises a number of technical difficulties, which are easily appreciated by inspecting the format to be followed. Alternatively, acceding countries may make a de minimis commitment in accordance with Article 6.4 of the Agreement on Agriculture, i.e. restrict 'yellow' domestic subsidies for a basic agricultural commodity to 5 per cent of its value of production (10 per cent in the case of developing country members). Both routes have been followed by recently acceded countries.

Accession negotiations with respect to agriculture have become protracted mainly because some applicants were not willing to commit themselves to cutting domestic support much more quickly (e.g. by making de minimis commitments) than current WTO members have done in the Uruguay Round negotiations. Similar problems arise with respect to agricultural export subsidies, where the Cairns Group of agricultural exporters has pushed for an early elimination. While the Cairns Group of countries have done so themselves (they tend to be highly competitive producers of temperate-zone agricultural products), once again this demand goes further than most OECD countries (and the EU in particular) have been willing to go in restricting their own export subsidies.

Services

The General Agreement on Trade in Services (GATS) represents a first step towards liberalising international trade in services. The agreement defines four potential modes of international service supply (cross-border supply, consumption abroad, commercial presence and the presence of natural persons); lists the general obligations of members (such as m.f.n. treatment, transparency, due process in domestic regulation and conditions for economic integration agreements); describes in detail the measures that are subject to members' market-access commitments (such as limitations on the number of service suppliers or on the types of legal entity that may provide a service); and lists various exceptions to GATS obligations (such as m.f.n. exceptions, subsidies, public procurement, balance-of-payments restrictions and national security).

Accordingly, WTO members' schedules of specific commitments on services consist of three parts: first, horizontal commitments that affect all sectors, for example with respect to the movement of natural persons or payments abroad; second, sector-specific commitments, which may be differentiated by the four modes of supply; and third, exemptions from m.f.n. treatment. While the GATS represents the general framework for liberalisation in services, negotiations since the Uruguay Round on financial services and particularly on telecommunications have led to substantial further liberalisation in these sectors.

Incumbent WTO members expect applicant countries, as a precondition for WTO membership, to offer economically meaningful commitments for at least a limited number of important service sectors. Across service sectors, access to financial services and telecommunications are of particular interest, not least because WTO members have themselves negotiated further liberalisation in these fields since the conclusion of the Uruguay Round. Because of the wide variety of sectors and the different modes of supply under GATS, it is difficult to provide a summary measure of the quality of the commitments agreed in recent accessions; a survey is contained in WTO 1999.

Reluctance to liberalise market access in services has been shown particularly by the transition economies among the applicants, where the service sector suffers from a double handicap. First, the central planning system has left many countries over industrialised but with underdeveloped service sectors. This was true especially for financial and business services, which are now crucial for the functioning of a market economy. With free entry, local service firms would often be overwhelmed by international competition. Second, the services that were provided in the past were usually produced under state monopolies. Hence, the opening of service sectors to international competition, particularly through direct investment by foreign suppliers (commercial presence), has met powerful political resistance.

At the same time, the international competitiveness of manufacturing industries depends increasingly on the firms enjoying access to high-quality services. Hence it is in the national interest of applicant countries (whatever resistance may be articulated by sectoral lobbies) to make economically significant commitments on service liberalisation. Where regional governments and non-governmental sectoral associations can control market access, it is also in the applicant country's interest to ensure that these entities do not undermine the free supply of services across regions in each country.

TRIPs

The TRIPs Agreement mainly obliges WTO members to implement certain specified procedures for the effective enforcement of a wide range of intellectual property rights: copyright and related rights, trademarks, geographical indications, industrial designs; patents, and the layout designs of integrated circuits.

The agreement builds upon and extends the provisions of the relevant international conventions (Bern, Rome and Paris; and the Treaty on Intellectual Property in Respect of Integrated Circuits).

The effective implementation of the TRIPs Agreement encounters problems in both former socialist and developing countries, because both (albeit for different reasons) traditionally tended to view intellectual property as a public, or partly public, rather than a private good. This is in contrast to the position of industrialised countries, which is closely reflected in the TRIPs Agreement, that intellectual property is a private good to be protected through appropriate legislation.

In transition economies, most legislation on intellectual property rights is of very recent vintage. Extensive advice received from the World Intellectual Property Organization (WIPO) has normally ensured that the new legal texts correspond to the provisions of the relevant international conventions as well as the TRIPs Agreement. However, effective enforcement, which is central to the TRIPs Agreement, depends on effective institution building in the legal system as a whole, which in turn is part and parcel of the difficult process of systemic transformation.

Many developing countries have traditionally been reluctant to extend full protection to intellectual property created mainly by firms in high-income countries, particularly if this would have enabled those firms to extract monopoly rents on the use of technologies deemed crucial for development (such as pharmaceuticals to combat diseases). Problems in accession negotiations have arisen both from the reluctance of some applicants to account fully for the private good character of intellectual property rights in their legislation and from difficulties with enforcement.

While the appropriateness of including intellectual property rights in the WTO framework has been questioned, TRIPs is now, for better or worse, part of the multilateral trading system. Applicant countries have no choice but to bring their legislation and law enforcement into line with the provisions of the TRIPs Agreement. This may be helped by the fact that the legitimate interests of developing countries are reflected in several relevant provisions. For example, national legislation may permit the use of intellectual property by third parties without the owner's consent for public non-commercial purposes such as disease control (Articles 30 and 31 of the TRIPs Agreement).

State Trading and Economic Transition

The WTO agreements assume implicitly that WTO members are market economies where economic agents are free to act according to commercial considerations. This is clear from Article XVII of GATT 1994, which stipulates that state enterprises, as well as enterprises with exclusive or special privileges, should be notified to the WTO and, furthermore, should be run solely in accordance with commercial considerations. The logic behind this provision is that enterprises directed by the state, or endowed with exclusive or privileged trading rights, can undermine a member's market-access commitments if they act on any other than a strictly commercial basis. Furthermore, the centrally planned economies that were members of GATT 1947 had special membership protocols that stipulated, inter alia, mandatory rates of import growth from GATT 1947 contracting parties; tariff bindings or similar commitments would have been meaningless in centrally planned economies.

State trading companies and exclusive trading rights are widespread in many applicant countries. Some transition economies among the applicants have made only limited progress in privatisation, so a large share of GDP is still produced by state-owned enterprises. In many countries, access to natural resources and the distribution of strategic commodities such as mineral ores or fuel are traditionally a domain of the state. In the case of Saudi Arabia, state trading companies are also instrumental in enforcing government controls on domestic sales of food and fuel products and setting domestic prices below international prices.

For accession negotiations, the crucial criterion for the compatibility of a given enterprise structure with WTO rules is not ownership but the actual behaviour of enterprises. If state ownership is still widespread, applicants need to demonstrate that enterprises effect their purchases and sales solely on commercial grounds. In spite of some evidence of restrictive practices, international trade has been one area of systemic reform in nearly all transition economies where progress has been relatively rapidly sustained. As a result, goods markets in transition economies have become more contestable, and the behaviour of existing enterprises is based increasingly on commercial grounds.

One indication of continuing progress in this direction is an active programme of enterprise privatisation. Typically, therefore, applicants have provided detailed information on their privatisation programmes during accession negotiations. Besides notifying state trading enterprises and those with exclusive rights or privileges, transition economies acceding to the WTO have committed themselves to reporting regularly on progress in privatisation (for example, annually in the case of Kyrgyzstan). While there are no well-defined criteria that a privatisation programme needs to meet in order to be considered as conforming with WTO rules, a regular reporting requirement improves the transparency of the incentive systems under which enterprises operate.

Developing country status

The WTO agreements acknowledge that developing countries may find it particularly difficult to fully meet WTO obligations with respect to trade liberalisation. Developing countries are therefore allowed greater freedom to restrict trade in exceptional situations, to withdraw from existing commitments such as tariff bindings in order to protect infant industries, or to provide domestic subsidies to agriculture. Other special provisions for developing countries relate to extended implementation periods for various obligations and to particularly poor, 'least developed' countries. With respect to market access for their exports, developing countries benefit from the 'enabling clause', which permits WTO members to grant imports from developing countries 'special and differential' treatment under the Generalised System of Preferences (GSP). Regional preferential trading arrangements between developing countries are permitted even when they do not meet the requirements of Article XXIV of GATT 1994.

All these provisions raise the obvious question of which countries are to be considered 'developing' and may thus benefit from more favourable treatment. Remarkably, criteria for developing country status have never been established either by the contracting parties to GATT 1947 or by WTO members. Whether a country is considered 'developing' depends on a unilateral decision of the trading partner (the US procedure for the GSP), or on membership in the Group of 77 (the EU procedure for the GSP), or on self-selection for other WTO purposes. Only the term 'least developed country' is clearly defined in the WTO context in accordance with the list drawn up by the UN.

In accession negotiations, developing country privileges such as under Articles XII and XVIII of GATT 1994 have been claimed by China in particular. This Chinese position was strongly resisted by current WTO members, not least because of China's relatively large share in world trade; resort to developing country privileges could have rendered Chinese market-opening commitments meaningless. In addition, the empirical evidence accumulated over the last several decades suggests that trade restrictions to promote infant industries or to protect the balance of payments provide no significant benefits to developing countries. Hence, applicants have nothing to lose from not using such measures.

The issue of extended implementation periods for developing countries is, in principle, more complicated. Developing countries (however defined) tend to possess limited administrative capacity, so extended implementation periods appear justified. However, in a formal sense, this issue will gradually die away because all implementation periods for new WTO members, as for current members, are calculated from the coming into force of the WTO Agreement (not from the date of accession to the WTO). This is now established practice and will most probably also apply to future accessions. In practice, therefore, all extensions to implementation periods for acceding countries are now subject to negotiation.

Key country perspectives

More than a decade has passed since the accession working party for China was established in 1987 under GATT 1947. Negotiations have dragged on tediously for a combination of reasons: China is a major exporter of traditional manufactures and these 'sensitive' exports are likely to grow further once restrictions stemming from the Multi-Fibre Agreement are removed (Uruguay Round Agreement on Textiles and Clothing). The consequent prospects for political trouble at home has hardened the determination of some current WTO member governments to push China, as a condition of WTO accession, towards a rather far-reaching liberalisation of market access for imported goods and services. With the large and growing size of the Chinese market, the liberalisation of market access is of far greater economic value to current WTO members than in the case of any other candidate country. However, pressure for rapid liberalisation was long resisted by the Chinese government, which pointed to the ongoing systemic transformation of the country with all its attending problems, in addition to China's low per capita income, which would traditionally have been accepted, in a GATT/WTO context, as justification for infant industry protection.

China had concluded bilateral negotiations on its terms of accession with Japan, Canada and the USA, but the agreement with the USA is probably the most far-reaching. Import tariffs are projected to fall from an overall average of 24.6 per cent in 1997 to 9.4 per cent by 2005, with an average of 7.1 per cent for some US priority products. Market access will also be enhanced in a wide array of service industries, including telecommunications, banking (with special provisions for auto finance), distribution and motion pictures. At the same time, the USA will be allowed to treat China as a non-market economy for another fifteen years in anti-dumping and countervailing duty examinations, and the USA may also apply a special safeguard mechanism (beyond that available under WTO rules) against imports from China for twelve years.

It remains to be seen whether these terms, which were described as particularly advantageous to US firms by the US negotiators involved, will be acceptable to China's other major trading partners, especially the European Union. While all commitments and concessions by China would automatically apply to all WTO members under the m.f.n. principle, other trading partners might emphasise market access in other products of particular interest to them and seek concessions similar in value to those obtained by the USA. Nevertheless, the bilateral USA-China agreement makes the successful conclusion of accession negotiations in the foreseeable future more likely.

Failure to conclude accession negotiations with China represents a critical, politically motivated accession barrier for Taiwan (officially called the 'Separate Customs Territory of Taiwan, Penghu, Kinmen and Matsu, Chinese Taipei'). Most current WTO members recognise the People's Republic as the only legitimate government of China and therefore accept the Chinese government's position that Taiwan should only accede to the WTO after China. This position cannot be justified from WTO rules, which only require members to be in full control of all trade-related policies, which is the case for Taiwan (as it is for Hong Kong, which continues to be a WTO member). Substantially, negotiations in the accession working party for Taiwan, which started in 1992, have been concluded without any major issues remaining unresolved.

It is at present unclear what political leverage China will gain on the Taiwanese accession to the WTO if it formally joins the WTO before Taiwan is given the chance to do so. In spite of growing trade and capital flows, political relations between the two governments remain difficult. However, a further politicisation of Taiwanese WTO membership would be detrimental to the cause of freer trade in a rules-bound world trading system. Together, China and Taiwan account for approximately half of the international trade of current

WTO non-members and for an even larger share of their combined population and GDP. Thus, their accession would bring the WTO a significant step closer to being a truly global institution.

Russia and other CIS countries

Accession negotiations with the larger CIS countries, especially Russia and Ukraine, have not progressed far and, significantly, little new ground has been covered during the last two years. This is in marked contrast to several smaller former Soviet republics (Kyrgyzstan, Estonia and Latvia) and Mongolia, which have managed to accede to the WTO since 1995.

In several ways, the slow pace of accession negotiations reflects the lack of progress made by most CIS countries in their transformation from centrally planned to market-based economic systems. First, accession to the WTO means that a very wide range of trade-related policies need to be formulated consistently. This has been particularly difficult to achieve for many newly independent states, whose administrative capacity is not well developed. Even if appropriate legislation is written (in which foreign advisors may play a helpful role) and passed, the subsequent implementation of WTO-consistent policies is still less than automatic. For example, Kyrgyzstan is still officially a member of a customs union with Russia, Kazakhstan and Belarus, although it has bound its tariffs on goods at very low levels that the other three countries say they find unacceptable.

Second, apart from unclear or conflicting legislation, even the implementation of existing, well-defined legal texts can be undermined by remnants of the old system such as pervasive and non-transparent state interference in the economy. For example, various types of barrier to internal trade have been documented in the case of Russia. In Belarus, direct administrative intervention in the management of enterprises is widespread, and the resulting lack of transparency could easily undermine any commitments on market access that Belarus might undertake. The fact that published legal texts may not represent the full range of measures that affect international trade inevitably complicates accession negotiations.

Finally, the larger CIS countries have been reluctant to commit themselves to significantly liberalising access to their markets. For example, the initial import tariff offer by Russia would do little more than let bound rates decline to the current applied level during a seven-ten-year implementation period. Such insistence on protection for domestic firms, which extends to many service industries, contrasts sharply with the demands for market-access liberalisation by current WTO members as well as the examples of countries that recently acceded to the WTO.

Least developed countries

Up to November 1999, six out of a total of thirty-four applicants for WTO membership were defined by the WTO as least developed (Bhutan, Cambodia, Cap Verde, Lao PDR, Nepal and Vanuatu), with another two regarded as least developed by UNCTAD (Sudan and Western Samoa). In addition, twenty-eight least developed countries (UNCTAD definition) are already WTO members. Apart from a low per capita income, common characteristics include geographical remoteness (i.e. large economic distance from major markets: island and landlocked states), reliance on a small number of export goods, mostly raw materials, weak administrative capacity, economic and ecological vulnerability, lack of market-oriented institutional infrastructure, and often political instability compounded by civil disorder.

For such countries, the gains from WTO membership in terms of enhanced access to exports markets for traditional products are probably small. Raw materials already enjoy low or zero import tariffs in OECD countries; domestic supply bottlenecks (including inadequate transport facilities) probably hamper export expansion more than policy-induced barriers on the demand side. Furthermore, although some raw materials have been subject to anti-dumping procedures by industrial countries, the least developed countries are typically not leading suppliers of specific raw materials and are therefore not much affected by anti-dumping measures.

Nevertheless, there are several good reasons for least developed countries to join the WTO and for current WTO members to support this process. First, WTO membership requires transparency and consistency in a wide range of trade-related policies. At the same time, WTO membership constitutes an external commitment to enforce these rules, which may create additional momentum in favour of necessary economic reforms. For example, in many of the least developed countries, vested interests collect monopoly rents from their control of strategic sectors such as minerals, fuels, and maritime and tourist resources. Such practices conflict with WTO rules on state trading, and the implementation of these rules would lead to enhanced transparency and an opening of markets. Furthermore, greater transparency would also encourage incoming foreign direct investment.

Second, WTO membership may induce the least developed countries to liberalise market access for imports, even if they are not necessarily required to do so as they benefit from 'special and differential treatment'. Not only will reducing the implicit tax on exports increase allocative efficiency and stimulate export diversification but market opening will also reduce the power of privileged traders, who have frequently been found to drive up import prices in the presence of high import tariffs.

Third, the WTO offers some protection against unilateral pressure from powerful importers as conflicts can be made transparent by invoking the dispute settlement mechanism. This is of particular relevance for the smaller least developed countries that depend on transit routes through the territory of a large neighbour with whom they also conduct a major share of their international trade (such as Bhutan and Nepal with India, or Cambodia and Laos with Thailand).

Policy Recommendations

Our discussion suggests that accession negotiations can be streamlined and accelerated if several rules of thumb, whose political and economic logic requires little justification, are obeyed. First, current members should not require applicants to liberalise market access substantially more than current members at a similar level of economic development have done. The essence of WTO rules is to ensure the transparency of national regulations and to provide for a progressive, negotiated reduction in the level of protection. There is no basis in WTO rules for requiring applicants to adopt an untypically low level of protection at the time of joining the WTO.

This rule of thumb could be questioned on the grounds that the outcome of USA-China bilateral negotiations vindicates those who call for a tough stance by current WTO members: the far-reaching liberalisation of market access agreed by China will be of long-term benefit to both China itself and its trading partners. However, this view would be short-sighted: First, accession negotiations with China could probably have been concluded long ago, with all the attendant benefits, had the US position been less out of touch with the trade regimes practised by other low-income countries.

Second, the bilateral USA-China agreement should not become a model for others, because it is heavily lopsided: despite the far-reaching Chinese commitment to trade liberalisation, the agreement allows the USA to continue to treat China as a non-market economy in anti-dumping proceedings and to subject imports from China to special safeguards. To treat China as a non-market economy is logically inconsistent because, as a WTO member, China will be subject to the restrictions on state trading contained in Article XVII of GATT 1994. Country-specific safeguards are fundamentally in contradiction with the m.f.n. principle, which requires safeguards to be applied without discrimination as to country of origin. The damage done to the WTO system by thus bending its rules cannot be justified by the short-term gains that US firms will derive from higher protection against Chinese competition.

As a second rule of thumb, applicant countries should fully accept the need for transparency in their trade-related policies and for the full implementation of relevant WTO rules. For many applicants, improvements in the transparency, coherence and consistent implementation of trade-related policies will represent the most important benefit of WTO membership. By contrast, market access for exports will only improve marginally, because most applicants already enjoy m.f.n. status with their trading partners and often benefit from preferential market access under the GSP

As a third rule of thumb, in negotiating their commitments on market access for imported goods and services, applicants should consider benefits and costs to their economies as a whole rather than narrow sectoral interests. More often than not, more liberal market access will be beneficial overall, even if it hurts particular sectors. This applies especially to liberalisation of trade in services. Underdeveloped business services industries represent an important obstacle to growth in manufactured exports, because access to high-quality services is a key requirement for successfully entering international markets for differentiated goods.

A fourth rule of thumb is that negotiations can be accelerated if clearer priorities are set for necessary changes in national legislation and practice. While important adjustments might well need to be made early on, extended implementation periods for non-essential items could be tolerated given the complexity of WTO rules and limited administrative capacity of applicants. At the same time, the setting of priorities would focus the accession negotiations more clearly and thus ensure that applicants are not required to 'shoot at moving targets' as new demands are brought up time and again by current WTO members.

6

Dispute settlement by WTO

Introduction

The WTO 's dispute settlement mechanism (DSM) is widely regarded as the jewel in the crown of the Uruguay Round and the very heart of the WTO. After all, as many members repeatedly pointed out prior to the reforms agreed in the Uruguay Round, what good are multilateral rules if they cannot be enforced? Five years of experience with the new DSM have indeed documented its central role in the multilateral, rules-based international trade regime. Despite the occasional (and understandable) misgivings felt by losing parties to a dispute, the DSM enjoys widespread support and is actively used, which in itself is testimony to its attractiveness.

However, it has also been revealed that procedural weaknesses in the dispute settlement process still exist. Perhaps even more importantly, a certain disenchantment with the DSM is also discernible as governments and citizens realise that perhaps they got more than they bargained for. The WTO 's dispute settlement has become the institution where the fundamental question of how to reconcile a rules-based international trade regime with the idea of sovereignty and the concerns of civil society presents itself time and again to politicians and trade negotiators and begs for answers that are not easily found.

Reform of the DSM was not at the top of any nation's negotiating agenda for the Millennium Round. This shows that, by and large, WTO member states are content with the system established in the Uruguay Round and certainly regard other issues as more pressing. Still, a review of the experience with the new DSM is of interest beyond the mechanism itself.

Experience with the new DSM

The new DSM provides WTO member states with an automatic right to lodge a complaint, entitles them to use an independent appellate review and offers them an effective enforcement mechanism. It provides a system that guarantees the framework of predictable, enforceable and generally stable rules for traders. The DSM is used actively by all member states, with the notable exception of the poorest, especially African, countries. From the birth of the WTO on 1 January 1995 up to mid-March 2000, there have been 191 requests for consultation concerning 149 distinct matters. For comparison, under the old DSM there had been only 207 cases in the entire period from 1948 to 1990. The higher number of cases also reflects the fact that member states have assumed more obligations under the Uruguay Round agreement. Countries have used the DSM responsibly: cases brought so far have merited the charge, i.e. cases have not been raised merely to harass other states. First, developing and smaller nations make more use of the new DSM than of the old. While this partly reflects the increasing role of developing countries as trading nations, it is also a sign of confidence in the system. If LDCs did not believe that the DSM would be powerful and impartial enough to guarantee their rights even against large trading powers, they would not try. Out of the 191 requests and 149 distinct matters, forty-nine and forty, respectively, have been raised by developing country members. In other words, about one in four cases sees a developing country as a complainant, which is below their share in world trade but higher than their share under the old DSM.

Second, the USA has been the most active user of the DSM, having been or being the complainant in fifty-five of the 191 requests. With a share in total requests of 29 per cent, the USA is well above its share of world exports, which in 1998 amounted to 17 per cent. On top of this, the USA has reserved its third party rights in almost every other major case. In particular, there has been no case against the EU where the USA has not been the complainant or a third party. (To be fair, it should be added that the EU is catching up rapidly: forty-nine complaints were raised by the EU, which represents a share of 25 per cent. However, this is less out of line with its share in world exports, which amounted to 20.3 per cent in 1998, than is the case with the USA.)

The active role of the USA is partly explained by the fact that it is the second largest trading power and has a diverse export base; it is therefore most likely to be embroiled in numerous trade conflicts. However, of greater importance is that this active use reflects domestic politics. At the end of the Uruguay Round, the US administration found it hard to sell the results to Congress for approval. There was great scepticism on the part of Congress as to whether the obligations that trading partners had subscribed to would actually be implemented. If not, Congress would have demanded that foreign markets be prised open using unilateral measures such as 'Super 301'. The administration therefore had to demonstrate that the multilateral system, and dispute settlement in particular, works. It did so by launching a number of cases where success for the USA was most likely (e.g. India-patents, Turkey-films, Korea-shelf life).

Third, a significant number of cases (forty-four) have been settled during the consultation phase or have been suspended. This is a high proportion of those cases that have moved beyond the consultation stage or have been settled (seventy-eight of the 191 requests are still in the consultation phase, which leaves 113 requests where a decision has been taken). This is easily explained by the fact that governments know that there definitely will be panel proceedings if they do not compromise. So if governments know that they are violating WTO rules they will avoid a highly publicised case unless domestic opposition to revoking the measure is too great. Consequently, it is not surprising to find that almost all complaints that are not settled during the consultation phase have gone all the way to the appellate body. Indeed, a negligible number of panel rulings (four) have not been appealed against.

Finally, as predicted, the EU has proved to be one of the more intransigent defendants, as is particularly obvious in the EU-bananas case. The EU has used all kinds of procedural trick to avoid implementing the panel's ruling, and the case has certainly exposed a major weakness of the new DSM.

The new DSM is much quicker and has a fixed time frame; however, the whole process still takes too long. It is unattractive for commercial interests to devote resources to drawing their government's attention to a trade violation by another country unless it can be expected to realise the commercial benefits from a repeal of those violations in a reasonable period. The EU-bananas case has amply demonstrated that member states can still engage in considerable foot dragging if they want to do so. The weakness exposed by this case is that there is no mechanism that compels a losing party to implement a panel's decision properly. By doing something, but not enough, a defendant can still drag out the whole process almost indefinitely, because the complainant must challenge the new, still non-compliant measure anew. This obviously erodes trust in the system.

The EU 's foot dragging is typical, and for a fundamental reason: while the new DSM automatically ensures that there is a ruling whenever a complaint is brought, the WTO has no ability to sanction offending actions directly or to compel compliance with rulings. This will remain so as long as there are nation-states. However, to deplore the lack of direct sanctioning power is to fundamentally misinterpret the nature of the DSM. It is not a strictly judicial process akin to national court proceedings. The power of the DSM rests in the fact that no country, no matter how powerful, is willing to bear the cost to its reputation of consistently standing outside the body of international trade law. As the EU has shown, it can take a very long time for countries to finally give in, but in the end, most are likely to do so. In any case, retaliation cannot be the aim of dispute settlement as it raises barriers rather than lowers them.

Besides, to regard the WTO as powerless ignores an important feature of the DSM: any country is allowed to lodge a complaint if it can demonstrate a prima facie violation of its legitimate export interests, even if these are only potential rather than actual. In its ruling on the EU-bananas case, the appellate body explicitly reiterated this provision (which already existed under the GATT), pointing out that the USA was entitled to act as a complaining party even though it was not an exporter of bananas itself. This provision allows for large coalitions to be built that are able to exert enormous pressure on a defendant. It is evident that this is of particular importance for smaller countries, whose sanctioning power is obviously limited because they account for only a small portion of the trade of large countries. By teaming up with other countries, considerable pressure can be generated, which in the end should discipline even the most intransigent defendant. More fundamentally, the provision underscores that WTO rules are designed to create competitive opportunities, not actual trade.

Diplomacy versus the rule of law

The WTO is an intergovernmental organisation and as such the scene of diplomatic conventions. It is not without reason that the dispute settlement understanding stresses that the prior aim of the DSM is to secure a positive solution to a dispute, i.e. a mutually acceptable solution arrived at in negotiations rather than imposed by the WTO. That the DSM walks the tightrope between diplomacy and the rule of law can be seen from five features:

- It is usually not appreciated that the consultation period is extremely important. It is not only an opportunity to arrive at an amicable settlement using the good offices that the WTO Secretariat is willing to provide in this phase. It is above all a phase in which a government can signal to the other party the difficulties that domestic political conditions and concerns cause. It is also a forum where compensation and concession can be exchanged away from the eyes of the public. The confidential nature of the consultation period is therefore extremely important. Of course, this clashes with demands for more transparency in the dispute settlement process. As member states do not have a legal obligation to notify the results, let alone the circumstances of their consultations, there is also some concern on the part of the WTO that smaller countries may be bullied into agreeing to positions that are not in their interests. These concerns certainly cannot be brushed aside easily but must be weighed against the advantages of an 'out-of-court' settlement. The fact that a large number of cases are settled amicably in the consultation period attests to this.

- WTO rulings have no binding legal force beyond the issue in dispute. The intention to establish coherence in WTO rulings will establish a body of case law on which future rulings can be based. However, in the absence of binding legal powers, panels and the appellate body possess some latitude to accommodate diplomatic considerations, which, indeed, they have been willing to use.
- No private party nor the WTO itself can initiate cases. It is up to member state governments to decide whether to pursue cases or not in due consideration of other political aims.
- Another instrument that the WTO uses to retain some political leeway is the doctrine of judicial restraint. When the new DSM was established, it was understood that the new body should not set law, merely interpret it. The appellate body in particular should restrict itself to ensuring the consistency of panel rulings and to rectifying legally false rulings; it should not engage in fact finding itself. As it has turned out, the appellate body has indeed frequently found fault with the legal reasoning of the panels. It could simply have stopped there, leaving it to the disputants to lodge a new complaint. But this would certainly have been unsatisfactory; it was therefore in the interests of member states that the appellate body engaged in some fact finding and law making. Indeed, one cannot but agree with the logic put forward by the appellate body that, in order to check whether the panel had arrived at a correct assessment of the facts, the appellate body had to assess the facts itself. What is more, some of the very broad cases brought before the DSM could not have been ruled on unless panels and the appellate body had been willing to interpret WTO regulations.

However, the appellate body has been very cautious in pushing the borders of judicial restraint. Obviously, this first responds to concerns by member states, some of which have already complained about the appellate body misusing its powers. But second, judicial restraint is also advantageous from the point of view of the appellate body itself preserving the diplomatic elements of dispute settlement. In the USA-shirts and blouses case, the appellate body explicitly endorsed the doctrine, thereby freeing itself from the obligation to rule on all legal issues raised by the disputing governments. Politically, this has the advantage that both the panels and the appellate body do not necessarily have to rule on issues that might be politically sensitive to either of the disputing governments.

- Another area where the WTO 's dispute settlement has shown a penchant for constructive ambiguity is the question of the legal effect of a panel report. Somewhat contrary to public perception (but certainly in line with actual experience as regards implementation of panel rulings), it is ambiguous whether a losing country has the obligation to bring the violating measure into line with the panel's recommendations or whether it may choose to compensate the victorious party and leave the measure intact. Responding to concerns about the loss of sovereignty voiced in the US Congress during the ratification process of the Uruguay Round agreement, US government officials, among others, have maintained that there is no legal duty to perform. In contrast, Jackson points out that there is a strong propensity towards the legal obligation of countries to comply with panel rulings. However, as he rightly emphasises, focusing on compensation and/or retaliation actually misses the point. It is not the threat of retaliation that induces countries to act but the credibility of the judgement rendered, which makes it politically and diplomatically difficult to ignore even if a country could theoretically get away with it.

Involvement of the private sector

Private sector involvement is a fashionable idea in international trade policy these days. However, this is where the similarities end. Whereas private sector involvement in international monetary affairs is mostly supported by the public sector and academic literature while being resented by the private sector, in dispute settlement private sector players actively seek greater influence, although the desirability of this is viewed with some apprehension by most governments and the academic literature.

Behind the idea of private sector involvement in dispute settlement is the notion that, like trade policy, dispute settlement is a two-level game. This is true in two respects: first, a government will only consider bringing a complaint to the WTO if domestic export interests draw its attention to treaty violations by nations; and, second, dispute settlement procedures must take into account that governments must be able to sell and implement the verdict domestically.

Complaints will only be lodged when domestic export interests exist and when those interests are able to exert pressure on their own government to use the DSM against another. This requires, first, that export interests are informed about the obligations other governments have taken on and, second, that they expect the return from an eventually successful verdict to exceed the cost of presenting the case to the government. The expected return in turn depends on the probability that the government pursues the case, the likelihood of winning the case and the expected pay-off when winning the case.

It follows that collective action problems may prevent cases being pursued if companies assume that the pay-off from prising export markets open would have to be shared with free riders. It also follows that the DSM will only be used to prise open large export markets. There is little incentive to sue against the violation of a WTO obligation by a small, poor country and indeed none of the least developed countries has been involved in a DSM case. It should also be noted that the long duration of dispute settlements reduces the pay-off, which is an added disincentive. Finally, it follows that the degree of responsiveness of a government to complaints brought by the private sector will have a decisive influence.

Should one draw from this that the private sector be given the right to sue other nations in the WTO directly rather than having to go via its own government? Certainly, this would go a long way towards raising the private sector's interest in the WTO and would also greatly enhance legal security for internationally active firms. It may also prevent governments tacitly colluding at the expense of the private sector. However, as mentioned above, unfiltered access of the private sector to the DSM may not be desirable from a political point of view. Raising trade disputes inevitably causes tensions with other countries. Given the fact that trade policy is but one policy target among many, governments must retain the right to decide whether the issue at hand is important enough to be pursued at a particular point in time or, indeed, at all.

Environment and Food Safety

Selling DSB rulings domestically has become a major issue ever since the USA-tuna case turned the attention of environmental groups to the existence and the importance of the WTO. The US government, in particular, has been under immense pressure to open the WTO to civil society. The administration has therefore proposed the enhancement of transparency of dispute settlement and giving interest groups direct access to the process. Several other governments, among them many from the developing world, have already indicated their fervent opposition to this idea.

The WTO itself has responded actively to public concerns. The appellate body has also gone out of its way to show its willingness to take into account the concerns of civil society by explicitly inviting private parties to submit their opinions: overruling the panel, the appellate body in the USA-shrimps case explicitly invited any interested party to comment on cases heard at the WTO by sending amicus curiae briefs. The appellate body noted that while a panel does not have to take such information into account, there was no reason not to allow the information to be sent. This statement was undoubtedly politically motivated, intended as a reaction to charges of a lack of transparency and democracy in the actions and structures of the WTO. Clearly, governments are no longer the only voices heard in WTO disputes. But to go beyond amicus curiae briefs and to admit private actors as parties to a case would seriously damage the DSM. Not only would it cause disputes to take longer to settle but it would also make cases more acrimonious.

No matter how skilfully the DSM walks the tightrope between diplomacy and the rule of law, the more clear-cut the case, the harder it becomes for panels and the appellate body to take the domestic political interests of the defendant into account. On the other hand, the greater the political fall-out, the more powerful the member state and the more support a defendant receives from other governments, the more likely it is that panels and the appellate body will seek a compromise. The appellate body has on several occasions accepted the overall panel ruling while substantially altering the reasoning. This was partly in order to ensure the legal consistency of WTO rulings, which is one of the tasks that the appellate body was created for; but it was also partly to enable the losing party to defuse political tensions at home by making the ruling more palatable.

The fiasco of Seattle has reinforced the impression that in the eyes of the public the DSM is not the 'jewel in the crown' that economists and lawyers tend to regard it as. Rather than seeing it as the triumph of the rule of law over power politics, the DSM is charged with undermining national sovereignty, damaging the environment, killing jobs and hurting people's health.

Exemplars of this are the EU-hormones, USA-shrimps and USA-gasoline cases. In the first of these, the appellate body did not change the verdict of the panel but substantially altered the legal reasoning. In particular and most importantly, it reversed the assignment of burden of proof: governments are allowed to set safety standards higher than international standards, subject to the limitation that member states must offer some scientific justification. It is for the complainant to prove that the higher standards are unreasonable. In the latter two cases, the appellate body addressed the sensitive issue of environmental concerns. In the USA-gasoline case, the appellate body explicitly stated that 'the ability of any WTO member to take measures...to protect the environment is not an issue'. It fact, the appellate body goes out of its way to stress that the protection of the environment is an important issue that member states should devote some energy to. In the USA-shrimps case too, the appellate body said that the USA had a legitimate aim but pursued this aim using the wrong, viz. unilateral, instruments. Beyond proving the WTO 's desire to display its willingness to take concerns about the transparency and accountability of the institution into account, both cases are typical examples of the appellate body's tendency to make rulings easier to swallow politically for the losing party while keeping the verdict itself intact. It is not only the appellate body but also member states (above all, the USA and the EU) that have shown restraint and displayed an interest in preserving the integrity of the

DSM. Cases that are highly politicised and that would have caused political uproar in the defending country have not been pressed hard. This is most obvious in cases such as Japan-Fuji and USA-Helms-Burton, which seem to have been dropped tacitly. Obviously, neither the EU nor the US administration (nor any other member state, for that matter) has an interest in damaging the DSM, even if they occasionally resent rulings against them (the stance of the US Congress on this is less certain, though). Governments seem to realise that while the DSM is at the heart of the WTO, it is also the potential source of conflict between member states and must therefore be handled carefully.

7

Reorganisation of WTO Decision Policies

Introduction

The first ministerial conference of the WTO was held in Singapore on 9-13 December 1996. The Singapore Ministerial Declaration issued at the end of the conference was based on a draft prepared in Geneva containing agreed text on all but some sensitive issues, including textiles and clothing, labour standards, investment, and competition policy. At the conference, an 'inner circle' composed of ministers from thirty-four of the WTO's 128 members took responsibility for arriving at an agreed text on the remaining issues.

The late evening session on 12 December was devoted to getting a consensus on the draft declaration, which had been finalised that day by the thirty-four-member inner circle. Most of the other ninety or so WTO members that had delegations in Singapore took the floor in turn, each making virtually identical interventions consisting of three points: first, they thanked the thirty-four members of the inner circle for their hard work; second, they said that although they had some reservations on certain points, they could join the consensus in favour of the draft declaration; and third, that the way in which the draft declaration had been prepared was undemocratic, unfair and disgraceful, that they were no longer willing to accept a decision-making process that always presented them with faits accomplis, and that they attached the highest priority to fundamentally revising the way in which important decisions are arrived at in the WTO. The conference chairman (Singapore's trade and industry minister) and the WTO 's director-general solemnly assured delegates that this topic would be put at the top of the work agenda when the members resumed their work in Geneva the following month. Few people with a knowledge of the inner workings of the WTO were surprised when this experience failed to produce any improvements in WTO decision-making procedures. Three years later, almost to the day, the venue shifts to Seattle.

Seattle, 3 December 1999. Largely as a result of wide differences between WTO members concerning the desirability of including a number of complex and sensitive issues on the agenda of a new round, coupled with a preparatory process in Geneva seriously compromised by the prolonged and acrimonious process earlier in the year of selecting a new director-general, WTO ministers arrived in Seattle with little or no agreed text for a 'Seattle Ministerial Declaration' to launch a new round of multilateral negotiations. Near the end of the conference, the usual way of arriving at decisions (as exemplified by the thirty-four-member inner circle in Singapore) broke down completely. This time, comments by countries excluded from the 'green room meetings' the name frequently given to inner circle meetings found their way into the popular press. For example:

'No one combs our hair in our absence', said a furious Ugandan, as the talks lurched towards collapse.

'From the very beginning, we saw that the process was flawed', said Charles Norris, trade minister of the Dominican Republic. 'We want to make sure that the WTO pays attention to our needs'.

'Green rooms aren't in the WTO Glossary. Which clause is it in? Which article?' demanded Nicchoro Mw'wanda, a technical expert for the Kenyan delegation.

A tendency to deny the seriousness of what had happened was already evident among some delegates soon after their return to Geneva. It is helpful, therefore, to 'document' the situation further by quoting from other press reports from Seattle and the immediate post-Seattle period:

Separate meetings of African and of Latin American and Caribbean countries Thursday night issued declarations threatening to quit the talks. 'African countries are being marginalised and generally excluded', read the African press release.

The 'green room discussions', the next level of debate, this time mostly between the rich countries, were excluding the poor. At least one African delegate was physically barred from attending.

The WTO's reputation for secrecy and elitism—criticised by outside protesters—was even roundly endorsed within its own ranks when many countries' delegates were excluded from the final round of talks held behind closed doors at the convention centre as leading nations tried desperately, but ultimately in vain, to hammer out a talks-saving pact.

The 'green room' format was activated, that is, a single committee limited to 25 countries designed to make rapid progress in a short space of time. Developing country delegates, the intended beneficiaries of the new policies of transparency and inclusion, were outraged. Denouncing a return to what they charged were practices that sought to marginalise them, they pointedly warned they were ready to block consensus. Delegates contacted late Friday night after the breakdown were sharply critical of the conference and its organisers, arguing that they once again had been excluded from the real sources of power.

The vast majority of developing countries were shut out of the whole green room process. They were not even informed which meetings were going on or what was being discussed. Ministers and senior officials of most developing countries were left hanging around in the corridors or the canteen, trying to catch snippets of news.

In the immediate aftermath of the failed ministerial conference, press reports quoted France, Japan and the WTO's director-general on the need for reform:

Tokyo—France and other nations agreed on the 'necessity of having a WTO ministerial meeting on its organization and procedures to make it more efficient, transparent and democratic.

Tokyo—Japan plans to appeal to its trade partners to set up an advisory organization within the World Trade Organization aimed at ensuring greater transparency in the world trade body's decision-making process, government sources said Monday.

Tokyo expects the advisory organization to consist of representatives from some 20 to 30 nations, including both industrial and developing nations, and make proposals to reflect the interests of various WTO member countries, they said. But any proposals put forward by the advisory organization would be nonbinding in view of the WTO's consensus-oriented decision-making rules, they said.

Auckland—'It is evident that the way in which the WTO member governments reached decisions needs to be re-evaluated', [Director-General Mike] Moore wrote in a column in the New Zealand Herald newspaper.

'All significant decisions are made on the basis of consensus. Clearly, this principle must be retained. You cannot have a system of rules which are enforceable by a binding disputes settlement system unless everybody accepts those rules,' he said.

'Final decisions are always made in the general council or by the ministerial conference. But the deal-brokering that takes place in any negotiation is impossible in a room with 135 ministers.'

'Everybody acknowledges the need to have smaller groups thrash out the compromises, but no one wants to be excluded from those groups.'

Paris—France will propose reforms to the World Trade Organization at the start of its six-month stint as EU president beginning in July, French Trade Secretary François Huwart said Thursday.

Several ministers said [after the disastrous meeting in Seattle] that a key reason for their inability to narrow their differences was the sheer size of the organization, which made it difficult to achieve democratic discussion without the proceedings becoming too unwieldy to make any progress.

Geneva—[Japan's International Trade and Industry Minister Takashi] Fukaya said Japan thinks it is useful to set up a small, informal forum in the WTO and that it is necessary to establish criteria for choosing the participants, such as trade volume, gross domestic product (GDP) and geography.

He also said it is important to ensure that the contents of its discussions are conveyed to non-participants.

And, at the end of March in Geneva:

Geneva – [WTO] delegates on Tuesday started discussing how to improve the body's decision-making process to avoid a repetition of the collapse last December of attempts to launch a new trade round.

At an informal session of the body's General Council, envoys from the 135-member WTO also confirmed their guiding principle of making all decisions by consensus, trade sources said.

The WTO will tackle the tasks of improving the 'transparency and efficiency' of decision making simultaneously, trade sources said. Participants also suggested organizing more regular contacts through video conferencing and discussed how to make information more easily available to all members.

Japan suggested having the contents of discussions at informal meetings reported to formal meetings, thereby giving all members opportunities to express their opinions.

The frustration and anger of countries routinely excluded from the green room meetings was not limited to their experiences in Seattle: 'Throughout the preparatory process [in Geneva] many of [the smaller countries] complained about semi-official meetings where the majority of Members could not participate'.

For the benefit of those readers who may be unfamiliar with the workings of the WTO, it is worth calling attention to three points. First, a very large proportion of the routine work takes place in committees, councils and other groups – that is, not in inner circles/ green rooms.

Second, the processes by which WTO members discuss, debate and negotiate issues is distinct from the organisation's reliance on consensus to adopt decisions (the members have made it very clear that they plan to keep the emphasis on consensus decision making). Any organisation with a large membership, and in which all groups, committees and councils are open to all its members, is going to have a problem functioning, regardless of whether it takes decisions by consensus or by simple majority. It is that particular problem the process by which WTO members arrive at the point where the entire membership is asked to adopt a particular decision.

Third, the question of reform of the WTO's decision-making process is not a North/South issue. Large and influential developing countries are regular participants in the green room meetings. It is, instead, a classic 'insider/outsider' issue, with the industrial countries and 'important' developing countries on the inside and all other WTO members on the outside.

The 'concentric circles' model

The inner circle/green room formula for creating discussion, consultation and negotiating groups small enough to function efficiently is known more generally as the 'concentric circles' model. An issue-specific inner circle of members, varying in number (for example, from eight to thirty-four) depending on whether the topic is narrow and of interest to only a few members, or broader and of interest to a larger number of members, functions as a discussion, debating and negotiating group. It either reports the results of its efforts to a larger circle of members, which then repeats the process and sends the results of its efforts on to the next wider circle of members, or it reports directly to the entire membership. In either case, at the end of the process the entire membership is generally asked to take a consensus decision on the recommendations coming from the more restricted circle(s).

Simplifying somewhat, the evolution of the concentric circles model can be traced partly to the fact that for much of the GATT's history, most developing countries were neither interested in nor encouraged to be interested in participating actively in the 'management' of the GATT system which meant that, for the most part, an inner circle could be constituted without excluding any (or at any rate, very many) of the members desiring to participate. When developing countries began to participate much more actively in GATT and then WTO activities, the concentric circles model became the organisation's de facto

way of dealing with a very fundamental problem: while membership in virtually every WTO body is open to all WTO members (currently 138), once the active participation in a group/committee exceeds a certain number (say twenty-five), discussion, debate and negotiation become increasingly cumbersome, inefficient and ultimately impossible. Organisations with a large membership traditionally deal with this problem by having an executive committee or board with a limited membership. As is discussed below, the IMF and the World Bank, for example, have twenty-four-member executive boards, and the UN has the Security Council. There is no corresponding formal body with limited membership in the WTO. The reasons behind the growing participation of developing (and transition) economies in GATT/WTO activities suggest very strongly that this trend can only intensify:

- The membership is growing. There were sixty-seven non-OECD GATT contracting parties in 1986, when the Uruguay Round was launched. At the time of the Seattle ministerial conference, the WTO had 103 non-OECD members, with thirty others at various stages in the accession process.
- Over the past fifteen years, a large number of developing countries and virtually all the transition economies have come to accept the view that a more liberal trade regime and fuller integration into the global economy must be a key part of their development strategies. And they understand that active participation in the WTO not only contributes importantly to both goals but also allows them to have a say in the evolution of the multilateral trading system.
- In the Tokyo Round, the GATT began to write rules for policies applied 'inside the border', and that process continued in the Uruguay Round (especially services, the protection of intellectual property, and sanitary and phytosanitary measures). At Seattle, delegates were discussing investment, competition policies, environment and workers' rights. Virtually all of these 'inside the border' issues are far more politically sensitive than policies applied at the border (tariffs, quotas and export subsidies), and as the GATT/WTO takes on these issues, countries are less and less willing to sit on the sidelines and let other countries do the work.
- Under the GATT, many of the rules governing trade-related policies were -officially or de facto optional for developing countries. Under the WTO's 'single undertaking', every member is subject to all the rules.
- Whereas under the GATT any member had the power to block a dispute settlement case that it objected to, that option no longer exists. WTO dispute settlement progresses automatically, and a final decision by the Appellate Body is binding and cannot be appealed against.

Against this background, it is hardly surprising that the current informal (that is, opaque) and exclusionary process for deciding which WTO delegations to invite into green room meetings has come under increasing pressure. Supporters of the concentric circles model stress that WTO members that have a strong stake in the outcome of a particular issue can gain access to the inner circle set-up to deal with that issue, and that such custom-designed, issue-specific groups are more likely to operate efficiently and effectively in the WTO context than 'fixed-membership' groups, such as the IMF and World Bank executive boards or the UN Security Council. This model is also viewed as contributing to the consensus approach to taking decisions. Members that were not in the inner circle, it is argued, will know that it was up to them to have made their claim for involvement earlier, rather than to block a consensus when the recommended decision is put to the entire membership. The concentric circles model heavily criticised by many WTO members in Singapore, and even more heavily criticised in the preparations for and activities in Seattle has confronted two kinds of problem. The less serious of the two, which should not be too difficult to resolve, involves the perceived lack of transparency regarding what takes place in green room meetings (since, for the purposes of this article, 'inner circle' and 'green room meeting' are largely synonymous, I will generally use the latter term). A better-organised dissemination of information and documents to non-participants in time for them to react and have an input will be a major part of any solution (perhaps the four deputy directors-general could play more of a role here). A much more serious problem occurs when the number of members demanding to participate in a green room meeting exceeds the limit imposed in order to ensure the group's efficiency and effectiveness. Certainly there are, and will continue to be, many issues that are of vital interest to only a limited number of WTO members. With equal certainty, we can be confident that as in Singapore and Seattle there will be issues of sufficiently broad interest to the membership that it will be necessary to exclude a significant number of interested members from the green room. Moreover, for the reasons noted above (the increasing membership, the WTO's growing involvement in politically sensitive policy areas), there is bound to be an increase in the number of instances in which it will be impossible to accommodate all the members desiring to participate in green room meetings. Although the concentric circles model, in one or another of its possible versions, continues to enjoy significant support among WTO members (for reasons that are explored below), it is very difficult to avoid drawing two conclusions from the preceding discussion:

- In those instances in which interest among WTO members in the issue at hand is sufficiently narrow that a green room group can be constituted without excluding any member desiring to participate, this model functions well and should continue to be used. In other words, as a venue for special types of discussion, debate and negotiation, green room meetings as well as bilateral meetings and all the other 'processes' that have been developed over the years in the GATT/WTO will continue to be used.
- In those instances in which it is impossible to organise a green room meeting without excluding one or more WTO members wishing to be included, continued reliance on the concentric circles model can only progressively damage the WTO's ability to function, erode its internal and external credibility, and push the organisation even further back in the direction of more and more issues being seen falsely and very unproductively in North/South terms. Clearly, the WTO needs a sub-group of members of an efficient size for the purpose of discussing, debating and negotiating draft decisions that can be put to the entire membership for adoption. What needs changing is the basis for putting together such a sub-group, for deciding which delegations will be in the room and which delegations will be excluded. The new basis needs to be one that is fully transparent, predictable and equitable in the eyes of all WTO members.

One option for creating such a new sub-group of WTO members is developed below. First, however, it will be helpful to take a brief look at two types of sub-group, one from the GATT and one from the IMF and World Bank.

GATT's experience with CG.18

The GATT's contracting parties established, on a temporary basis, a body that in a limited way resembled an executive board.

Called the Consultative Group of Eighteen (CG.18), it was made a permanent body in 1979 and held its last meeting in 1987, as the Uruguay Round moved into high gear. In its report to the GATT Council recommending that it become a permanent body, the CG.18 stated:

It is strongly believed in the Group that the GATT should have at its disposal a small but representative group which would permit existing and emerging trade policy issues to be discussed in confidence among responsible officials from capitals, and thus facilitate an effective concentration of policies in the trade field.

The CG.18, which met from two to four times a year, was not expected to deal with management issues ('How do you run an organisation where every committee is open to every member?') but rather to fulfil the major countries' desire for an issue-oriented consultative body of a manageable size whose participants would be senior officials from capitals.

Any thought of using the CG.18 as a rough blueprint for designing a new group that would move into action whenever a green room meeting could not accommodate all WTO members wishing to participate would have to begin by acknowledging that the CG.18 suffered at least from today's perspective from a serious transparency problem. GATT contracting parties that did not have a seat on the CG.18 were barred from the meetings and did not receive CG.18 documents. A near-exclusive reliance on officials from capitals would also be unworkable, since the new group presumably would, from time to time, need to meet much more frequently than the CG.18. On the other hand, given the stated desire of WTO members to continue to rely on consensus decision making, any new group should follow the CG.18's fundamental principle of not taking any formal decisions but rather only making recommendations to the entire membership.

'Executive director's' model

A board of twenty-four executive directors is the principal decision-making body in both the IMF and the World Bank. The IMF's Executive Board meets at least three times a week, while the bank's board of Executive Directors normally meets twice a week. Although there is provision for weighted voting in both organisations, both try as much as possible to work on the basis of consensus.

Eight executive directors represent individual countries on the IMF board (China, France, Germany, Japan, Russia, Saudi Arabia, the United Kingdom and the United States), and sixteen represent groupings of the remaining 174 members. The same eight countries have individual seats on the World Bank's board of executive directors. In the IMF, thirteen of the sixteen groups that share a board seat have between six and fourteen members, one has only four members (two of which are India and Bangladesh), and two groups of African countries have twenty and twenty-two members, respectively. The country composition of the sixteen groups of World Bank members is very similar to that of the sixteen IMF groups.

Considering that the WTO is a rules-based organisation whose raison d'être is the provision of legally binding constraints on what countries can do in the area of trade-related policies, and that it is a one-country, one-vote organisation (in contrast to the weighted voting in the IMF and the World Bank), it is very unlikely that WTO members would be willing to create a board of executive directors that could take decisions that bind the entire membership.

'WTO consultative board'

The option developed in this paper for a new sub-group of WTO member countries involves creating what might be called a 'WTO consultative board'. It would not be necessary to have predetermined, regularly scheduled meetings, since the board would normally meet only when a green room meeting could not accommodate all WTO members wishing to participate. The design and operating procedures of the new board would draw on the strong points of both the CG.18 and the IMF/World Bank boards while avoiding the shortcomings (from the perspective of the WTO's needs) of both.

As with the CG.18 (and the concentric circles model), the WTO consultative board would not be empowered to take decisions that bind the general membership. It would consult, discuss, debate and negotiate, but its output would be limited to recommendations put forward to the entire membership for approval/acceptance. And, as with the executive directors model, the board would be a formal part of the WTO organisation chart, and its composition-which members have a seat at the table and when would be fixed (that is, predictable), presumably with the largest traders having individual seats and the remaining WTO members divided into groups, each with one seat that is shared between the members of the group on a rotating basis.

Minimising the exclusivity of a WTO consultative board

A major challenge would be to minimise the exclusivity of the board in the eyes of members that would have a seat at the table only on a rotating basis. The fact that the board could not take decisions would be vitally important from this perspective. Surely the other major factor would be transparency. I believe it would be crucial, as regards both substance and political acceptability, to make the work of the board fully transparent and accessible to all the members.

All WTO consultative board documents could be made available simultaneously to all WTO members. One could imagine an arrangement whereby members that were not at the table would be able to watch the deliberations of the board in their delegation offices on secure closed-circuit television. Another option, the pros and cons of which are hard for me to judge, would be to set up the meeting room with a table and chairs in the centre for the current members of the board, surrounded by seating for all the other WTO members, who would be free to observe but not to intervene in the proceedings. Along with increasing the political acceptability of such a board, a high degree of transparency along these lines would facilitate subsequent efforts to get a consensus because countries that were not members of the board would be aware of the nature of the 'give and take' involved in arriving at a decision to recommend to the entire membership.

Another way to minimise the exclusivity of the board, or at least the perceived down side to the exclusivity, would be to use broad similarities in interests and viewpoints on trade-related issues as the basis for composing the groups of WTO members that share seats. In this way, the members of any particular group—when it was not their turn to be at the table—would feel that at least their group's seat was occupied by a country that shared many of their concerns and priorities in the trade area. Composing the groups on this basis would not be an insurmountable task.

Size of a WTO consultative board and allocation of seats

The question of how many seats the board should have would be very contentious. One option for getting around this politically charged issue would be to follow the practice of the IMF and the World Bank, each of whose sub- groups for discussion, debate and negotiation that is, their respective boards has twenty-four members.

Allocating seats would surely be the most contentious part of the task of creating a WTO consultative board. One approach would be to base seat allocation on some combination of three criteria: share of world trade and share of world GDP, 'tempered' by the fact that the WTO is a one-country/one-vote organisation (the board, of course, would never vote because it could not take formal decisions). Whatever the criteria, it is very likely that the United States, the European Union and Japan which together account for nearly half of world merchandise trade (excluding intra-EU trade) would have individual seats. The members of ASEAN could share a seat, as could members of other regional groupings. And so on.

As in the IMF and World Bank boards, the groupings could be self-selected and could have the option of 'self-changing' their composition, say once every two years. The countries in each group could also be given the freedom to decide how often to rotate the occupancy of the group's seat at the table. In general, the principle could be to allow as much flexibility as possible in order to accommodate a variety of situations (which can change over time).

A decision to have twenty-four seats would mean that the groups that share seats in the consultative board would have, on average, noticeably fewer members than the groups that share seats on the IMF' and World Bank boards, for two reasons: WTO membership is likely to remain below that of the IMF and the World Bank (182 and 181, respectively) for some time; and a WTO consultative board would presumably have fewer single-country seats than the eight single-country seats in the IMF and World Bank boards (for example, individual European Union member countries, three of which occupy individual country seats on the IMF and World Bank boards, would not be candidates for seats on the WTO board because the EU speaks for its fifteen members in the WTO).

The members of ASEAN share, among themselves, responsibility for covering WTO activities. In the case of the General Council, responsibility for covering the meetings and, when needed, intervening on behalf of the ASEAN group, is rotated among the members every six months. When it is the turn of one of the newer members of ASEAN, which is less experienced in WTO matters and may have fewer human resources available, the other ASEAN members help that country to carry out its responsibilities (preparation of interventions and so forth) vis- a-vis the General Council. Among other things, this is an important learning process for those newer and less experienced members.

There is no reason why each of the groups sharing a seat on a WTO consultative board should not function in much the same way. Cooperation between the self-selected group members to support whichever member currently occupies the seat would help to compensate for the shortage of experienced professionals in Geneva and in support units back home which plagues so many of the middle and lower-income WTO members. It would be an important learning process and morale builder for the officials involved, both in

Geneva and in their own capitals. Domestically, the much more active involvement of these countries in important WTO activities remember, they include the ninety or so members that have been routinely excluded from the green room meetings would raise the profile of the WTO, and trade policy in general, in government circles and in the private sector. Governments that have been slow to recognise that commercial diplomacy has replaced political diplomacy as the critical priority for countries pursuing economic development would be encouraged to reallocate scarce human resources away from activities, abroad and at home, that contribute little or nothing to the country's economic development and put those resources to work on the WTO.

The latter point calls attention to one of the most damaging aspects of the green room model, with its opaque basis for deciding which delegations are allowed into the room and its de facto permanent exclusion of more than three-quarters of the WTO membership. It is only human nature that if a country's senior trade officials the Geneva ambassador and the cabinet minister responsible for trade feel marginalised by the WTO, they will be inclined to marginalise the WTO at home. A new kind of sub-group of WTO members along the lines of a WTO consultative board could go a long way towards solving this problem.

There are likely to be two overlapping sources of opposition to the proposal that a formal WTO consultative board be created to consult, discuss, debate and negotiate whenever a green room meeting cannot accommodate all WTO members that wish to participate.

First, there is very little doubt that the strongest and most vocal opposition to replacing the concentric circles model will come from a majority of the twenty to thirty members that are big enough to demand entry to any inner circle/green room they are interested in but not big enough to demand an individual seat on the new board. (A good idea of which delegations are in this category can be obtained by subtracting the United States, the European Union and Japan from the twenty-five countries reportedly invited to the green room meetings in Seattle, or from the thirty-four countries that drafted the Singapore ministerial communiqué. Bear in mind that the fifteen individual members of the European Union do not participate in the green room meetings.) Not long after their return from Seattle, at least some delegates from countries admitted to the Seattle green room meetings were privately denying that the green room model had been seriously discredited by what happened in Seattle the same process of 'denial' that helped to torpedo the post-Singapore deliberations on decision-making reform. They argue that the press and isolated WTO delegations greatly exaggerated the extent to which the need to exclude many WTO delegations from the green room meetings had created serious problems.

It is important not to underestimate the amount of hard work undertaken by the regular participants in WTO green room meetings virtually all of whom are drawn from the same group of twenty to thirty WTO delegations or the extent to which the individuals involved have contributed to the functioning of the WTO. At the same time, the countries excluded no doubt view the group of essentially permanent green room participants as an exclusive 'club' that has assumed responsibility for 'running the WTO'. Regular green room participants may not think of themselves as a club, but there is little doubt that many of them will exhibit a very club-like desire to protect their prerogatives against demands or proposals for reform that involve sharing those prerogatives more widely among the membership. And while it is undoubtedly true that many of the ninety-plus excluded delegations often are less well briefed on the issues, there is very much a 'chicken and egg' aspect to the situation why should a delegation bother to use up scarce human resources to be fully prepared on the issues when it knows from experience that it will not be consulted on them?

A second source of opposition and one that might find one or more of the United States, the European Union and Japan allied, at least to some degree, with other green room members is the argument that it would be politically impossible to obtain a consensus on a proposal to replace the concentric circles model with a formal new body along the lines of a WTO consultative board. Without putting it to the test, there is no way of knowing whether or not this assertion is correct. What does seem clear is that if the ninety or so routinely excluded WTO members decide that they are no longer willing to be a part of the implicit consensus supporting the green room model, it will become totally unworkable.

A corollary of these observations is that, since they are the ones who are routinely excluded, it should not be difficult to convince the ninety or so medium-sized and small WTO members of the advantages of having a formal and fully representative alternative to the concentric circles model, one that can be activated whenever relying on a green room meeting would involve excluding WTO members. Sharing a seat may not be ideal, but it is a lot better than never being allowed into the room.

A discussion of which countries are likely to oppose or support the creation of a WTO consultative board would be incomplete without a brief mention of the response of many of the major countries to the signing, in Seattle, of the agreement establishing the new Advisory Centre on WTO Law (the only success in Seattle). The centre is a new international organisation that is completely independent of the WTO. The rationale for creating the centre is simple and compelling. While large and wealthy WTO members can afford to have experienced trade lawyers as regular full-time members of their delegations, this option is not available to most middle and lower-income developing countries. They must turn to very expensive outside lawyers when they need qualified legal assistance. The main purpose of the new centre is to help to correct this imbalance by providing subsidised legal assistance to developing countries in other words, to help them to defend their legal rights in the WTO.

Developed countries were asked to join the agreement and provide financial support. However, for several of them the usual keen interest in a 'level playing field' seems to evaporate when it comes to a country's ability to enforce its WTO rights. For example, the European Union (which strongly opposed the creation of the centre), the United States, Germany, France and Japan all firm believers in the rule of law at home and in a rules-based trading system did not sign the agreement in Seattle. Although this development does not necessarily imply that the countries that failed to support the creation of the new centre would be 'unenthusiastic' about the creation of a WTO consultative board and the more active participation of the middle and lower-income developing countries in WTO activities that would result the implications are not particularly encouraging.

Predictability, transparency and above all legitimacy

Since any new sub-group of WTO members responsible for discussing, debating and negotiating an issue would be used only when a traditional inner circle/green room could not accommodate every member wishing to participate, the predictability, transparency and legitimacy of the new 'sub-group process' would be critically important. From this perspective, the IMF and World Bank boards have two very important characteristics: the board is a formal part of the organization 's structure, and every member country's 'participation rights' in the board are fully transparent and predictable. In other words, because the IMF and World Bank boards are integral parts of the organizations each is a formal part of the organisation chart they have predictability, transparency and, most important of all, legitimacy. This contrasts with the green room model or for that matter, with any new informal, ad hoc WTO group that countries might be considering as a cosmetic response to the events in Seattle (and Singapore) which lacks predictability, typically suffers from serious transparency problems and has none of the legitimacy that comes from being a formal part of the institution's organisational structure (witness, for example, the quote from the Kenyan delegate in Seattle).

This is why I believe it would be a very serious mistake if the perceived political difficulty of agreeing on a formal change in the WTO 's structure led member countries to create yet another informal ad hoc 'group' or 'forum'. Any informal group or forum risks collapsing in acrimony and distrust at the first serious confrontation because it would have no 'structural strength' and would suffer from a 'deficit of legitimacy'. The new group must be a formal part of the organization on the WTO organisation chart and connected by a solid line, not a broken line, to the rest of the chart.

Conclusion

The risk facing the WTO is that the political challenge of obtaining a consensus on a fundamental reform of the decision-making process along the lines proposed in this paper, coupled with the GATT/WTO 's traditional pragmatism, will create a nearly irresistible momentum to attempt to 'muddle through'. If the member countries and the director-general give in to this temptation, the prospects for the WTO to realise its full potential will be very bleak indeed.

As for the ninety or so WTO members that are routinely excluded from green room meetings, the choice is clear. If they want to see the creation of a formal and fully representative sub-group of WTO countries along the lines of a WTO consultative board, where each would have the opportunity to occupy a seat at the table periodically, and when they were not in the seat they would know that it is occupied by a fellow group member that shares their views on many issues and would listen to them when they want to make an input, they will have to fight for the change. The countries that have grown accustomed to 'running the show' at the GATT and now the WTO are not going to hand it to them on a silver platter.

8

Investment in the WTO

Introduction

Shortly after the failure to reach agreement on the launch of a new round of WTO negotiations at the ministerial converence in Seattle in December 1999, it is not clear when or whether a new comprehensive round of WTO negotiations will begin. The inclusion of investment in WTO negotiations will in part depend on there being a comprehensive agenda. If WTO member countries opt for a more modest round of negotiations based on those policy issues on which consensus already broadly exists, then the prospects for any of he 'new commercial' agenda items, including investment, will not be good. Inclusion of new issues is more likely in a multilateral round that provides for trade-offs over coverage.

It is not really accurate to describe investment as a 'new' issue, since it has been on the GATT and WTO agenda for some time. The Havana Charter of the International Trade Organization (ITO) included provisions on investment. Even the General Agreement on Tariffs and Trade of 1948 covered some aspects of investment policy, but these were not applied until the United States brought a case against the Canadian Foreign Investment Review Agency (FIRA) in 1983. Before the 1980s, all GATT contracting parties maintained controls on capital flows and foreign direct investment, so there was no interest in seeking to apply the GATT rules. From the late 1970s onwards, however, there has been a progressive shift towards more liberal investment policies, starting with the United States and Britain in the late 1970s, followed by Japan and the rest of the European Union member states in the mid-1980s, then Scandinavia and a number of leading newly industrialising countries (NICs) in Latin America. Flows of foreign direct investment increased significantly in line with this liberalisation. During the 1980s, US efforts to include investment in the coverage of the Uruguay Round had only limited success, due to the opposition of some leading developing countries and less than wholehearted support from EU Member States. As a result, the Uruguay Round covered only trade-related investment measures (TRIMs).

Independently of the GATT talks, all OECD countries and a large number of NICs had made the shift to liberal investment policies by the end of the Uruguay Round in 1993. This liberalisation involved removing controls or screening of incoming FDI in manufacturing, more liberal regulation of services, such as financial services and telecommunications, and privatisation of 'sensitive' or 'strategic' sectors, such as transport and energy, which had been excluded from investment liberalisation even under the OECD codes.

The modest results of the Uruguay Round on TRIMs were therefore seen by those in governments and the private sector, which constituted the rather narrow policy-making community in international investment regimes, as being at odds with the liberal paradigm that prevailed at the time. There was little interest, let alone opposition, from the non-governmental organisations that were to figure in the failure of negotiations on a multilateral agreement on investment (MAI) in the OECD in 1998. The prevailing and apparently uncontested view in 1994 and 1995 was therefore that there was an opportunity to agree on a strong set of rules for investment that would ensure the rules kept pace with market and policy developments and rationalise the patchwork of bilateral, plurilateral, regional and multilateral rules that had been put in place in the absence of a comprehensive multilateral regime.

This broad consensus among OECD countries concealed differences, particularly between the USA and the EU, over what the regime should cover and in which forum it should be negotiated. The United States pressed for negotiations in the OECD, with the aim of extending the model of the North American Free Trade

Agreement (NAFTA) rules on investment to the multilateral level. The NAFTA model offered progressive liberalisation, high standards of investment protection and dispute settlement that included provision for investor-state action. The European Union favoured multilateral negotiations within the WTO on the grounds that the main barriers to investment were in developing countries and that these needed to be involved in negotiations from the start rather than being asked to sign up to a fait accompli negotiated by OECD countries.

The outcome of these differences was a two-track approach, with negotiations beginning in the OECD on an MAI in May 1995 and the establishment of a working group on trade and investment in the WTO at the Singapore ministerial conference in December 1996. The MAI negotiations stalled in 1997 and finally failed in 1998. The EU's hopes of including investment in the WTO agenda were lost, along with the new round, in the debacle of the Seattle ministerial conference in December 1999.

What is the next step? Should investment be included in a new round of the WTO, if and when it is launched? Is there likely to be enough support for an ambitious agreement on investment? If not, what elements of the menu of topics included in regional, plurilateral and bilateral investment agreements should be included in modest negotiations? I will argue that there is a need for a multilateral framework for investment within the WTO, because the existing patchwork of investment rules cannot, in the long run, provide the predictability and confidence that is needed for FDI flows to continue, which is in the interests of both investors and host countries.

Multi-layer patchwork of investment rules

The current debate is not whether there should be international rules on investment or not, but whether there can and should be a consolidated framework of principles accommodating the existing patchwork of rules at plurilateral, regional, bilateral and multilateral levels. This patchwork of rules already constrains national investment policy options and grants rights to and imposes far fewer obligations on international investors.

what has been proposed for future agreements at whatever level.

Before looking at this patchwork of rules, it is helpful to summarise the provisions of existing investment agreements and

A menu of provisions in investment agreements

Definition of investment: can be broad asset-based definitions, including intangible assets such as intellectual property; or narrow definitions limited to FDI and excluding portfolio investment.

Transparency: information on host country rules and regulations affecting investment and/or requirements to list exceptions to provisions of agreements; is thought to assist liberalisation by obliging governments to defend restrictions on investment.

National treatment and m.f.n. status: core elements of all agreements that require non-discriminatory treatment of FDI, if national treatment is provided for investors (i.e. new incoming FDI) this is equivalent to right of establishment.

Bans on performance requirements: partial or total bans on conditions attached to investment, such as local content, export or trade balancing requirements.

Control of investment incentives: provisions banning or controlling subsidies and tax incentives.

Movement of key personnel: right of entry into a host country for the managerial and technical staff needed to support an investment project.

Monopolies and competition/antitrust policy: provisions aimed at ensuring that national monopolies do not deny access for FDI or at ensuring that national competition law and practice ensure contestable markets.

Coverage/sector exceptions: coverage defined by top-down or negative lists, which list all sectors or horizontal measures (such as FDI screening) excluded; or bottom-up or positive lists, which list everything covered.

Exceptions for regional integration agreements: provisions for preferential or regional agreements, such as the EU or NAFTA.

National security exemptions: exemptions for control of investments or acquisitions contrary to security/foreign policy interests.

Investment protection: provisions against uncompensated expropriation or controls on payments or other capital transfers. Can include de facto expropriation and measures having the equivalent effect to expropriation, i.e. denying the investor the benefits of his/her investment.

Corporate governance: provisions that seek to ensure that market practice, such as cross-shareholdings, does not effectively block FDI.

Dispute settlement: provisions to enforce agreements, which may be state-state (only governments can initiate actions) or the more intrusive investor-state (private companies can challenge governments).

Social and environmental policy: provisions aimed at preventing regulatory arbitrage as investors choose locations with low standards of employment or environmental protection, such as policy harmonisation or approximation. These may involve obligations on investors rather than obligations on states.

The OECD instruments

The most extensive multilateral rules on investment can be found in the OECD codes and instruments. Work on investment issues in the OECD dates from the establishment of the organisation in 1961 but more specifically from 1964, when the codes on liberalisation of capital movements and current invisible operations were adopted. These codes are binding on OECD members and require the progressive liberalisation of controls on capital movements. The basic approach of the codes has been to improve transparency by requiring member countries to notify any 'reservations' or exceptions from free movement of capital. Until the late 1980s, these reservations were quite extensive and covered sensitive sectors such as energy and telecommunications as well as horizontal controls or screening of inward and outward investment. Once barriers to investment were identified, peer pressure, in the shape of reviews of exceptions in OECD committees, then served as the 'enforcement mechanism'. In practice, this meant that the pace of liberalisation was really determined by each national government. However, the codes had a 'ratchet effect' in that they precluded any reintroduction of an investment control or liberalising measure. The codes have developed and been strengthened to cover more issues:

- In 1984, the codes were strengthened to effectively require OECD countries to offer the right of establishment to signatories of the codes, subject to the remaining reservations, although investors still have to comply with host country regulations. At the same time, there was a debate about whether national monopolies, such as in telecommunications services, were compatible with liberal investment policies, but the right to allow such monopolies was retained.
- In 1986, changes were made requiring notification of 'reciprocity' provisions in national regulations (the conditioning of access for FDI upon equivalent access to the home country). Existing reciprocity rules were 'grandfathered'.
- In 1990, there was a review of the national treatment instrument (NTI) by the OECD. The NTI originates from the so-called Declaration and Decisions on International Investment and Multinational Enterprises of 1976, and together with the MFN provisions in the codes provides for non-discrimination between OECD countries. The NTI employs the same approach as the codes in that it ensures transparency through notifications of exceptions to national treatment. Progressive liberalisation is then encouraged through peer pressure. However, unlike the codes, the NTI is not binding, so new laws can be introduced that discriminate against inward investors. The 1990 review led to efforts to strengthen the NTI by making it binding and extending its scope. The negotiations failed because of US-EU differences over the inclusion of sub-federal level government (sought by the EU) and provisions on regional preferences. The NTI review only succeeded in strengthening procedural rules that made notification of exemptions to national treatment binding.

The OECD approach is therefore based on transparency, requiring notification of reservations or exceptions to m.f.n., non-discrimination and national treatment requirements. Transparency facilitates peer review of exemptions from national treatment and m.f.n. (primarily in the Committee on International Investment and Multinational Enterprises). Together with the 'ratchet mechanism', which precludes the re introduction of an exception to the right of establishment once it has been removed, this has contributed to a progressive liberalisation. But the pace of liberalisation has been determined predominantly by OECD governments acting unilaterally. Failure in the 1990/91 negotiations on a binding NTI did not mean the end of debate in the OECD. Work continued on the feasibility of what was at the time called a 'wider investment instrument' that would consolidate and strengthen the codes and NTI and address unresolved issues. The negotiations on an MAI in 1995 can therefore be seen as a continuation of existing OECD work.

Regional Agreements

The treaties establishing the European Community offered de jure national treatment and the right of establishment anywhere within the Community, with a very limited number of exceptions, such as national security and broadcasting. Notwithstanding these rules, there was no de facto right of establishment due to national regulation of services, investment screening and controls in manufacturing and an absence of contestable markets. During the 1980s, liberalisation by member states, competition in markets and the liberalisation of capital controls through an EU directive in 1988 brought about more or less complete liberalisation of investment within the EU. With the exception of France and Greece, this liberalisation was extended erga omnis, at least to other OECD countries. This left monopolies or oligopolistic market structures in such sectors as telecommunications, gas distribution, power generation and distribution, postal services and rail and air transportation, which have been addressed through specific-sector directives and European competition policy. European competition policy has also been deployed to control the use of investment subsidies or incentives to attract FDI. Within the EU, there has been a harmonisation of environmental and to a lesser degree social and tax policies, which has reduced, but by no means removed, regulatory competition between investment locations in the EU. This approach to investment has been adopted by countries neighbouring the EU, especially those that have negotiated or are seeking accession and that are therefore obliged to adopt the European acquis.

Much of the impetus behind negotiations on rules for investment has come from North America, and from the USA in particular. As early as 1970, ideas had been emanating from the United States for a 'GATT for investment'. The United States pushed the idea of GATT coverage of investment in the Consultative Group of 18 in 1981, and at the (failed) 1982 GATT ministerial conference the USA pushed for a code on investment in the GATT covering, among other things, 'performance requirements'. The USA was motivated by a desire to remove controls such as those operated by the Canadian FIRA. In 1982, the USA brought a case against Canada before the GATT claiming that the FIRA infringed, among others, GATT Article III.4 (national treatment). The GATT panel on the case ruled in favour of the USA but limited the effective coverage of GATT by also arguing that developing countries could use GATT Article XVIII.c (government assistance to promote economic development) to justify the imposition of performance requirements. Such limitations motivated US interests to press for stronger GATT rules on investment, pressure that ultimately led to the inclusion of TRIMs in the Uruguay Round negotiations.

Not surprisingly, in the light of the FIRA case, the 1988 Canada-USA Free Trade Agreement (CUSFTA) provided for national treatment of investment and the phasing out of export and production-based performance requirements. It also eliminated Canadian screening of all but large investments. For its part, the USA had no general controls on investment other than those for reasons of 'national security', which were indeed revised in the 1988 Omnibus Trade Act. Given the USA's role in global security, it has retained considerable discretionary power to block inward FDI on grounds of national security. Concern about the potential for abuse of such provisions as a means of blocking foreign takeovers in 'sensitive' sectors for commercial reasons has resulted in a desire to tighten rules, in the MAI negotiations, for example. This is especially true when, as in the case of the United States, there is no independent review of decisions taken by the Committee for Foreign Investment in the United States (CIFIUS), the inter-agency US committee that makes judgements on such questions. In line with the approach taken by OECD countries, the CUSFTA excluded certain sensitive sectors, such as energy, mining, air transport and fishing, from the national treatment obligation. The automobile sector was also excluded from the obligation to remove performance requirements because of the desire to retain local content rules.

The NAFTA extended the approach used by the CUSFTA to include Mexico and provides for national treatment at a federal and state/province level and m.f.n. status. Performance requirements are prohibited, and the agreement explicitly cites export performance requirements, domestic content, local preferences, trade balancing requirements (with regard to both exports and foreign exchange), domestic sales requirements, the obligation to transfer technology, and exclusive sales requirements. The granting of incentives depending on location of investment is possible, but these cannot be conditional upon performance requirements, such as using a certain percentage of local products. There are also provisions on investment protection, including expropriation and transfer of funds. One whole section of the NAFTA is concerned with dispute settlement, which provides for investor-to-state actions. The dispute settlement procedures are detailed and include use of the arbitration procedures under the ICSID (the World Bank-based International Centre for Settlement of Investment Disputes) and UNCITRAL.

The NAFTA uses the top-down, negative list approach to coverage, with Mexico understandably having the longer list of exceptions. Both Canada and Mexico have exceptions for cultural industries. As in the case of the EU and as discussed below, the GATT the NAFTA has specific provisions for financial services and telecommunications. In broad terms, the NAFTA provisions offer a considerable degree of liberalisation over time. They require governments to ensure that public monopolies comply with the NAFTA and that market strength through regulated monopolies is not used to distort competition in other sectors. But there is no NAFTA level competition policy that can work to ensure that private restraints on access do not replace public regulatory restrictions. The first draft of the NAFTA negotiated by the parties in 1992 included only passing reference to labour and environmental issues. But the negotiation of NAFTA provoked considerable controversy among labour and environmental organisations in the United States. These saw NAFTA as a threat to the high standards of labour and environmental protection that they had worked years to establish. Lobbying from these NGOs (non-governmental organisations) influenced opinion in Congress, particularly among Democrats, who look to such groups for votes and funding during elections. Congress then blocked ratification of NAFTA until 'side agreements' on labour and environmental protection had been negotiated by the incoming Clinton administration. The NAFTA undoubtedly provided a model for the USA in future investment negotiations because it embodied US business interests in high standards for liberalisation, investor protection and investor state dispute settlement. It has perhaps been overlooked that the NAFTA also possibly provided a model for NGOs seeking to ensure that labour rights and environmental standards are not undermined by investment agreements.

GATT and investment

The General Agreement on Tariffs and Trade was designed for trade in goods. Investment provisions in Articles 11 and 12 of the Havana Charter were lost with the International Trade Organization (ITO). Even when the ITO was being negotiated, there was a reluctance to extend the scope of trade agreements to include foreign companies for fear that this would undermine sovereignty. The GATT's narrow coverage of goods and like-products traded meant greater simplicity in the application of national treatment and m.f.n. Reviews of the GATT's coverage of investment in the 1950s, 1960s and even 1970s did little to change this view.

Trade-related investment measures in the Uruguay Round

The idea of including investment in the GATT re-emerged during the 1980s. The progress made in the OECD led some countries to favour extending this to the GATT But ideas to include investment in the Uruguay Round negotiations were opposed by some leading developing countries, which feared that GATT rules would limit their ability to use investment policy as an instrument of development. At the launch of the Uruguay Round in Punta del Este in September 1986, a compromise was reached with the effect that only those investment measures that had an effect on trade, or trade-related investment measures (TRIMs), would be the subject of negotiations.

It was further agreed that the negotiations would first examine how the existing GATT operated with regard to TRIMs and only then elaborate, as appropriate, further provisions that may be necessary to avoid such adverse effects.

US negotiators, backed by leading US multinational corporations in sectors such as information technology and in the service sector in general, were the ones making the demands in TRIMs they sought the prohibition of fourteen TRIMs. At the other end of the spectrum, India and Brazil argued that developing countries should continue to have the right to use performance requirements as legitimate instruments of development policy, and that the GATT already covered key TRIMs. The EU assumed an intermediate position, favouring the prohibition of a shortlist of five TRIMs, some of which, such as local content requirements, were arguably already covered by the GATT, with a longer list being 'actionable' (i.e. subject to complaint) under the GATT. This position was also adopted by Japan and some of the NICs. Japan was mainly concerned about local content requirements in the USA and EU. Confirmation that the GATT already covered certain TRIMs was not sufficient to satisfy the Americans, but developing countries opposed any extension of GATT rules. As a result, there was no agreement on investment for four years during the Uruguay Round. Even in the run-up to what should have been the concluding ministerial conference in Brussels in December 1990, there was still no text on investment/TRIMs. Following Brussels, views converged towards a compromise position, which enabled a draft TRIMs Agreement to be included in the so-called Dunkel text of December 1991, the draft final agreement of the round as a whole.

The Dunkel text and final agreement required all TRIMs contrary to the GATT to be notified to the GATT. An annex to the agreement provides a non-exclusive list of TRIMs that fall foul of the existing GATT. This includes local content and trade balancing requirements (contrary to Article III:1); trade balancing requirements (contrary to Article XI:4); and foreign exchange restrictions and export requirements (contrary to Article XI).

Developed countries had to eliminate such measures by 1997, developing countries by January 2000, and the least developed countries by 2002 (Article V). Finally, the agreement establishes a committee on TRIM's to review progress towards the objectives of the agreement. Any dispute is subject to the general dispute settlement provisions of the WTO, which means state-state only. There was also provision for a review of the agreement after five years. This, along with the question of whether some developing WTO members should be given longer to implement it (as well as other Uruguay Round agreements), now forms part of the WTO 's ongoing work post-Seattle.

From the point of view of those who demanded a comprehensive agreement on investment, the TRIMs Agreement was well short of the target and did little more than agree to prohibit measures that had been contrary to the GATT for fifty years. This lack of satisfaction in progress in the GATT/WTO had an important bearing on the post-Uruguay Round debate, in which the USA opted for a plurilateral OECD forum for the next push to establish comprehensive international rules for investment. However, before looking at the post-Uruguay Round debate, we must first complete the patchwork of agreements by looking at the General Agreement on Trade in Services (GATS) and bilateral investment treaties.

Other WTO rules governing investment

In addition to the TRIMs Agreement, other WTO agreements have a bearing on investment. The most important of these is the GATS, which is concerned with opening markets in services, but because a presence or establishment in a market is important for access to many service sectors, effective access can only be assured through direct investment. In fact, the GATS envisages four modes of supply for services, one of which (mode 3) is through the establishment of a branch or subsidiary. The GATS also includes obligations on host country regulators to treat foreign-owned companies in the same way as nationally owned companies (national treatment) after establishment.

In contrast to the OECD codes and regional agreements such as NAFTA, the coverage of GATS is determined by a combination of the positive (or bottom-up) listing of sectors covered by the general agreement and of the negative listing of exceptions within each of the sectors covered. This makes for a complex set of schedules determining coverage, but on balance coverage is less comprehensive, which is what developing countries wanted. As in regional agreements, certain key service sectors, such as financial services and telecommunications, are covered by sector-specific agreements, which go further than national treatment and require a degree of policy harmonisation. In other words, in these key service sectors the GATS represents a considerable degree of multilateral rule making.

Comparing the GATS agreement with the menu of provisions of investment agreements, we find that although national treatment, m.f.n. and transparency are all present, as indeed are exceptions for regional agreements (Article V, GATS). There are no provisions on investment protection, and dispute settlement is state-state rather than investor-state. Even if the coverage of GATS were to be extended, those interested in these aspects of investment agreements would find the GATS a weak agreement. As the GATS has been signed by all WTO members, it is unlikely that there will be revisions that include such investment protection measures.

The WTO agreement on trade-related intellectual property rights (TRIPs), on the other hand, does provide some elements of investor protection, at least with regard to intellectual property. As one of the major motivations for FDI is to exploit the intellectual property of the investing multinational company, protection against the 'expropriation' of intellectual property rights is of considerable importance in some sectors. However, in line with other WTO agreements, there is no investor-state dispute settlement provision in the GATS, so those investors seeking such means of ensuring their intellectual property is not 'expropriated' may still prefer bilateral investment treaties that include such provisions over TRIPs.

Bilateral investment treaties

In the absence of comprehensive and effective multilateral investment agreements, bilateral investment treaties or BITs have grown to fill the vacuum. This has occurred mainly during the 1990s, when two-thirds of the total of 1,513 BITs agreed up to 1997 were concluded. BITs were initially used by a number of OECD countries to ensure more predictable climates for investment in developing economies. From the host country perspective, BITs helped to promote the confidence of investors and thus growth in inward FDI. More recently, the developing and transition economies have begun to negotiate BITs among themselves. Indeed, of the 153 BITs concluded during 1997, most were between developing countries or developing and transition economies.

The substantive elements of BITs vary from treaty to treaty, but generally speaking they tend to use a broader definition of investment than that used in multilateral investment agreements. Investment is often equated with property, so both moveable and immovable property are covered, as are ownership rights, claims on money and intellectual property rights. Most BITs include provision for m.f.n. and a majority national treatment, but the formulation of these rights varies from BIT to BIT. Almost all BITs include investment protection provisions covering expropriation, transfer of funds and in many cases general provisions that protect investment from any impairment of the use or disposal of assets. These provisions mean that host state regulations that reduce the value or ease of access to assets could be covered by BITs. However, only a minority of BITs, mainly those concluded by the United States, cover performance requirements and provisions ensuring the temporary right of entry of key personnel. Finally, almost all BITs include dispute settlement provisions, usually providing for arbitration, and they provide reference to ICSID and/or UNCI-TRAL and ICC (International Chamber of Commerce) procedures.

Summing up, judging by the growth in investment agreements at various levels over the past twenty years, it would seem that there is a demand for international rules governing investment. In the absence of a comprehensive international or multilateral agreement, there has been a growth of bilateral and regional agreements, which tend to be of a 'higher standard', offering greater protection for investors. This has resulted in the basic elements of the OECD rules being extended to developing and transition countries via bilateral agreements, or implemented through more binding regional agreements. Rule making has taken place at all levels: bilateral, regional, plurilateral (OECD) and multilateral. In each case, the rules have used different combinations of the menu of provisions in investment agreements offered above, so that although the agreements have common elements, there is a considerable degree of inconsistency across agreements. This inconsistency creates uncertainty for investors and may have a dampening effect on investment. Rules developed on one level have also tended to provide models for other levels. For example, there appears to be some evidence that the approach developed in the USA for bilateral agreements helped to shape the CUSFTA and NAFTA. The NAFTA, in turn, was seen as a model for the 'multilateral' OECD negotiations on an MAI.

Post-Uruguay Round debate

In the period following the conclusion of the Uruguay Round in 1993/94 there was a consensus in the international investment policy community (largely consisting of government officials and private sector experts) on the desirability of new negotiations on a comprehensive multilateral agreement on investment. It was felt that this offered a window of opportunity for a regime change. The expectation was that the negotiations on investment would not be controversial. However, as noted above, the Uruguay Round negotiations were a disappointment for those pressing for effective, multilateral rules of a high standard. There was also support among the policy makers for the liberal view that 'investment could provide the next great boost to the world economy following the powerful impulse given by the removal of trade barriers during the Uruguay Round'. But before this could happen, there was a need to establish a more predictable environment for FDI through the replacement of the patchwork of partly contradictory agreements that had grown up with a multilateral agreement.

Although there was a consensus on the desirability of further negotiations, differences of view remained over the right forum (WTO or OECD) for negotiations, and sharp differences continued over some of the issues that contributed to the collapse of the 1991 OECD negotiations. As will be shown below, the cohesive nature of the international investment policy community was irreversibly changed from 1997 onwards when labour, environment, development and other NGOs chose to enter the debate. The choice of forum pitted the United States against the European Union. The USA pressed for negotiations in the OECD on the grounds that the kind of high-standard multilateral agreement that it wished to negotiate could not be negotiated anywhere else. The NAFTA model that the USA was basing its negotiating position on called for investor protection extending to de facto expropriation provisions, investor-state-based dispute settlement and a top-down (negative list) approach to coverage. The USA also wanted to have another attempt at prohibiting European discrimination against US film and audio-visual products and services, which escaped GATS disciplines thanks to the EU sticking to its GATS Article II exemption for this sector. Developing country members of the WTO were not ready to negotiate on these issues and were probably not even ready to consider the extension of the list of performance requirements sought by the USA. By building on past OECD work, most recently the feasibility work on a 'wider investment instrument' undertaken in the OECD from 1991, the USA believed that a high-standard agreement could be concluded, which would then be open for non-OECD countries to sign.

The European Union preferred negotiations in the WTO on the grounds that most barriers to EU investors were in developing countries and not in the OECD. As set out in a European Commission discussion paper, the balance of opinion in the EU favoured the WTO because it was more inclusive and because it was unrealistic to expect developing countries to sign up to a fait accompli negotiated in the OECD. Negotiating in the WTO inevitably meant a more modest agenda, which would in any case make it easier for the EU to maintain a consensus among its member states. The EU agenda therefore included transparency, national treatment and m.f.n., as well as effective dispute settlement. Issues such as a ban on further performance requirements and expropriation provisions were seen as secondary. The EU sought continued exclusion of 'cultural industries' and exceptions for regional preferential agreements while pressing for the inclusion of 'sub-federal' government. The states and provinces of the USA, Canada and Australia are not generally covered by OECD or WTO rules, and the EU wanted to ensure that they would be covered by any investment agreement. Finally, the EU wanted to deal with the issues of the extraterritorial reach of national laws governing investment. The longstanding European opposition to the extraterritorial reach of US law had been further strengthened by US efforts to deny European investors in the United States rights that they could expect under OECD and WTO agreements.

MAI negotiations

Despite its preference for the WTO as a forum, the EU agreed to begin negotiations in the OECD. The OECD ministerial conference in May 1995 launched the MAI negotiations and set 1997 as the target completion date. From this it was clear that any OECD text would be concluded before WTO negotiations could realistically be started, since the next WTO ministerial conference (at which a working group on trade and investment was established) would not be held until December 1996. The view in the OECD at the time was that there had to be an ambitious agenda to make the MAI exercise worthwhile. Presumably, this meant that the effort and risks involved in a new negotiation would have to be justified in terms of results that improved on the existing OECD instruments and WTO agreements. The mandate for the MAI was to negotiate a comprehensive and fully binding agreement at the highest standard in every respect. This meant that the negotiations had to succeed where the earlier OECD negotiations in 1991 had failed in agreeing on a binding coverage of national treatment. In order to achieve this, the negotiations had to deal with the unresolved issues, including, for example, coverage of sub-federal government, which the US administration could not deliver in the face of Congressional opposition but which the EU sought. An ambitious agenda also meant resolving the issues of carve-outs for cultural industries and regional preferential agreements, on which the EU was not ready to move, and finding compromise wording for security exemptions from the agreement. On top of resolving these old issues, the negotiations had to agree on a range of new issues. In practice, the MAI negotiations had to find a consensus on all the issues listed on our menu of potential provisions for investment agreements. Progress was made with this ambitious agenda until 1997, when a draft negotiating text was produced. This showed progress on many fronts:

- the definition of investment was to be a broad asset-based one including FDI and portfolio investment;
- there was to be national treatment and m.f.n. for investors and rules for transparency;
- coverage was to include all sectors and all levels of government, but subject to 'a balance of commitments' (in other words key issues of coverage such as the cultural exclusion

and sub-federal government would depend on the final package);

- there were to be additional disciplines for performance requirements, privatisation, monopolies and key personnel;
- investment protection was to include provisions on expropriation and measures having an equivalent effect to expropriation; and
- dispute settlement was to be based on state-state and investor-state actions.

However, a number of key issues, such as 'cultural exclusions' and definitions of the security exemptions, continued to cause difficulties. It has also been suggested that governments began to get cold feet about conceding so much control over investment policy in a multilateral agreement.

During 1997, opposition from NGOs began to grow, and the posting of the draft negotiating text on the Internet provided a rallying point for organised labour and environmental groups with concerns about the agreement. These NGOs feared that the agreement would undermine national standards of environmental protection and labour conditions. There was also opposition from development NGOs, which feared that developing countries would have little choice but to sign the agreement, and in doing so they would significantly limit the scope for development policies. The negotiations and the OECD were damaged by claims that the MAI negotiations, which would have far-reaching effects on a range of interests, had been conducted in secrecy. This is inaccurate, since the negotiations had been launched with public statements by the OECD ministers. But as noted above, the policy community that was engaged in the negotiations was a fairly select group. In defence of those responsible for negotiating the MAI, few people outside business and even few people in business had paid much attention to previous OECD negotiations. The negotiators probably continued to assume that there would be little public interest.

With hindsight, it is perhaps surprising that the NGO response was not anticipated. The NAFTA negotiations had generated considerable opposition from labour and environmental groups, and if the NAFTA could be seen as a model for investment negotiations in the MAI, why could the negotiation of the side agreements not be seen as a model by labour and environmental groups? The opposition from development NGOs was anticipated in the sense that it was known that LDCs would resent being excluded from negotiations and then presented with an agreement to sign. Perhaps the fact that the NAFTA and the results of the Uruguay Round had been ratified in the US Congress and other parliaments led negotiators to believe that there would be little opposition. Perhaps negotiators were too busy listening to private sector interests, which favoured proceeding with the negotiations. But the political masters of those negotiating the MAI were certainly surprised by popular opposition to the MAI, which had been coordinated by NGOs at an international level via the Internet. Such opposition meant that the negotiations could turn out to be a vote loser, with the result that governments had to act.

In an attempt to defuse the opposition, concessions were made to environmental and labour interests, in particular, with general wording inserted into the draft agreement covering these issues. But these amendments did little to placate NGO opposition, which saw the MAI as promoting globalisation in the interests of multinational companies. However, the inclusion of social and environmental provisions was not welcomed by multinational companies, which opposed binding obligations on themselves. Furthermore, difficulties in finding consensus on some of the substance of the agreement meant that the agreement would have to be watered down (from the high standards sought by business) if it was to find a consensus among governments. Together, these developments reduced the value of the MAI for international business, so support among the agreement's main supporters ebbed away. Growing doubts on the part of the governments negotiating the text, opposition from NGOs and a weakening in support from business combined to bring negotiations to a halt in the spring of 1998. A six-month pause was agreed, during which opposition only grew. In the end, the French government, under strong pressure from public protest, formally withdrew from the negotiations just before they were due to resume in October 1998, which had the effect of killing the MAI. The report produced by a French parliamentarian on the MAI provides an indication of the kind of watering down that was being called for in the public debate. The Lalumiere Report argued that France should withdraw unless a number of conditions were met. These included a more limited definition of investment (excluding portfolio investment and asset-based definitions), removal of provisions on investor-state dispute settlement, more limited provisions on expropriation (which would effectively preclude the inclusion of the provisions on de facto expropriation), an abandonment of the 'ratchet', and limits on the coverage of TRIMs (so that the MAI would only extend the prohibition of TRIMs agreed in the Uruguay Round to services). The recommendations of the report were that the negotiations be started anew and that developing countries be included. In effect, this meant that the WTO would be the forum and that the scope of the agreement would have to be much more modest.

Investment in the WTO

Thanks in large part to the EU, a WTO working group on the relationship between trade and investment was established at the Singapore ministerial conference in December 1996. Given the continued opposition from many developing countries to anything that might be seen as the first step towards comprehensive negotiations on investment in the WTO, and the prevailing US view that a WTO agreement on investment would be too weak to be of any value, the remit of the working group was constrained to studies. The mandate given to the group was that it should consider (1) the implications of the relationship between trade and investment for developing countries and economic growth; (2) the economic relationship between trade and investment; (3) the existing instruments and activities regarding trade and investment; and (4) identification of common features, differences, advantages and disadvantages of entering into bilateral, regional and multilateral rules on investment. The work of the group between 1996 and 1999 provided little by way of convergence of views.

In the preparatory work in Geneva on the agenda for the Seattle ministerial conference and the draft communiqué to launch the WTO Millennium Round, it was the EU that remained the main party demanding the inclusion of investment in an ambitious round. In the Council of Europe conclusions of October 1999, the Council called for negotiations to begin in the WTO on investment. While the conclusions do not indicate a great deal of detail concerning the

Council's mandate to the Commission on this issue, they do appear to limit investment to FDI (excluding negotiations on portfolio investment) while calling for negotiations to address access to investment opportunities, non-discrimination and protection of investments. The United States was opposed to including investment and was seeking a more modest agenda that reflected its own interests. Given the legacy of the MAI, the US administration wanted to avoid provoking US labour, environmental and anti-globalisation NGOs in agreeing to negotiate an agreement that US business was convinced would not be worth the paper it was written on. Leading developing countries such as India also continued to actively oppose including investment in the WTO agenda, while most LDCs simply had more pressing objectives, such as improving access to developed country markets. The Geneva process failed to make any real progress on the investment issue, as was the case with other sectors, although the draft communiqué, which was all in square brackets (meaning that it had not been agreed), appears to reflect the general EU line as reflected in statements by the Commission.

In Seattle, the EU, jointly with Hungary, Japan, Korea and Switzerland, tabled a common paper. This also reflected the EU 's objectives and its assessment of what sort of investment coverage would be acceptable to the LDCs. The paper called for a multilateral framework for investment in the WTO that would be based on non-discrimination, ensure transparency, address the relationship between WTO rules and those of the OECD and regional and bilateral agreements, seek progressive liberalisation using a positive list approach, address policies and practices not covered by the existing WTO, and exclude investor-state dispute settlement and take into account developing country needs. This text was presented to the negotiating group on 'new issues', but the group made little progress on this or other issues in Seattle as most negotiating effort went into addressing agriculture. It should be stressed that the WTO framework, proposed by the EU and supported in the end by about fourteen WTO members, was very different from the agreement proposed in the MAI. But there can be little doubt that the fact and the manner in which the MAI failed contributed to the absence of support for the inclusion of a framework for investment on the WTO agenda.

Future prospects

There is certainly a rational case to be made for rules on investment to keep pace with developments in global markets in order to provide a stable and predictable environment for investment. If this case holds for goods and services, it should hold for investment, which is a major element in the internationalisation of markets. There is also a growing risk of conflict between bilateral, regional, plurilateral and multilateral rules governing investment. On the other hand, FDI is increasing anyway, despite the patchwork of rules that exists today.

At present, there is no consensus in favour of a WTO framework for investment. In the absence of such a consensus, the alternative approach of using existing WTO agreements, particularly the GATS, is likely to be followed in the short to medium term. As noted above, the GATS covers much the same issues for services as a WTO agreement on investment would. As much of the growth in FDI is in services, an extension of the GATS to include more sectors and perhaps some more horizontal rules provides an alternative route to coverage of investment through probably stronger rules than would have been possible in a new overarching framework agreement for investment. As the controversy over investment has not (yet) affected services, this option is likely to be attractive to some negotiators. In the field of goods, the parallel option of extending the coverage of the TRIMs Agreement seems somewhat less likely, given the limited agreement achieved only recently in the Uruguay Round. Finally, in theory, the TRIPs Agreement could also be used to provide further protection for intangible assets of investment. But this option will be limited by opposition from development NGOs and LDCs and the disinclination of multinational companies to reopen the intellectual property rights debate at the present time. Making use of existing WTO agreements would not deliver the investor-state dispute settlement that is sought by the USA, but this is probably too intrusive into national sovereignty anyway. The risk with such an approach is that if these alternative WTO agreements are to be used to at least partially fulfill the aims of an investment agreement, why should there be less opposition in these negotiations than to a negotiation on investment? If the opposition stems from concern about WTO rules intruding into national regulatory competence, why should it be easier in GATS than an investment negotiations? Is this really in line with the spirit of transparency? Is it feasible for investment to be included on the WTO agenda? The legacy of the MAI makes the likelihood of being able to negotiate anything approaching an ambitious agreement highly unlikely.

Governments, in particular the US government, have become wary of the issue and are not generally willing to risk political capital to negotiate an agreement that would be short of what is desired by the private sector. If investment is to get on to the WTO agenda, it will have to be in the shape of a modest package along the lines of the paper tabled by the EU and other states in Seattle. This would have to focus on transparency, the core principle of non-discrimination. Coverage would have to be limited to FDI and not include, for example, portfolio investment or broad asset-based definitions of investment as used in the MAI or NAFTA. Dispute settlement would have to be limited to state-state actions, because it is not on the cards that a consensus of WTO members would agree to the precedent of private rights of action under the WTO. Such an agreement would do little more than provide a multilateral framework for what will probably continue to be unilateral decisions to liberalise. But then this has been the practice in investment since the 1960s.

If the agenda for investment in the next round has to be of such a modest nature, it may be better to continue work on investment in the working group on the relationship between trade and investment with a view to preparing the ground and public opinion for inclusion in the round after next. This would be especially appropriate if the next round takes the form of a more modest mini-round than the one envisaged or proposed by the European Union in Seattle. In such a modest round, it is unlikely that new issues, on which there is no broad consensus on the need for stronger WTO rules, will get on to the agenda. In any case, a consensus first needs to be achieved on the scope of a WTO framework for investment. This may be as easily achieved in the working group as in formal negotiations.

The difficulty with this pragmatic approach is that in the absence of any consolidated multilateral framework, the patchwork of investment measures will continue to expand. This could at some point in the not too distant future begin to create real tensions between the different regimes. Therefore, there remains a need to develop a clear multilateral framework, although for such a framework to have any effect, it must discipline or at least provide firm guidelines for bilateral, regional and plurilateral agreements. While the pace of liberalisation will be decided by WTO members unilaterally, any WTO agreement would also have to be binding in the sense of preventing the reintroduction of discriminatory policies that had been liberalised. If national policies can switch between liberalisation and control, there would be no predictable climate for investment and arguably a greater risk of governments using deregulation to attract investment. In short, the model for a WTO framework agreement is perhaps not the NAFTA, with its high standards, and certainly not the MAI, but the approach of the earlier OECD codes.

9

Trade Remedies: Reform and Action

Introduction

The average number of countries routinely initiating anti-dumping cases has more than quadrupled, from five in the late 1980s to more than twenty today. The average annual number of cases has almost doubled between the late 1980s and late 1990s. Since 1993, seven new users (Argentina, Brazil, India, Korea, Mexico, South Africa and Turkey) have initiated as many cases as the five 'old' users. Although quite dramatic, these figures still underestimate the true extent of the problem. They ignore the fact that the average number of tariff lines covered by anti-dumping cases has increased during the 1990s. They ignore the many 'reviews' of previous or existing cases, which extend initial measures almost systematically and indefinitely (the 'sunset' clause being quite ineffective).

The protectionist drift of anti-dumping may be dramatic, but it should not hide a similar evolution among some of the many trade remedies allowed by the international trading regime. Some remedies have a broad intent and scope: general exceptions (GATT XX and GATS XIV), provisions dealing with changes in commitments (GATT XXVII and GATS XXI), and balance-of-payments provisions (GATT XII and XVIII, and GATS XII). Others have a strong sectoral focus: Article V of the Uruguay Round

Agreement on Agriculture or Article VI of the Agreement on Textiles and Clothing. Lastly, regional agreements provide their batch of similar instruments, with often weaker disciplines (e.g. the safeguard provisions included in the agreements between the EU and Central European countries).

As a result, reforming all the trade remedies existing in the WTO regime (not only anti-dumping) is an urgent need amplified by the following considerations. The coming round will have to deal with industries skilful and powerful enough to have escaped the progressive trade liberalisation brought by the last eight rounds (textiles and clothing, steel, farm and food products). Developing countries will increasingly be under the same pressure to renege on their commitments as industrial countries, since the next round is likely to see a narrowing of the gap between their applied and bound tariffs. In the absence of robust negotiating techniques, liberalisation of services will require the 'safety net' of an 'emergency safeguard' clause. As a result, there is a need for both the establishment of principles guiding a bold strategy for reform and for a progressive implementation of these principles.

A Strategy for Reform

There is an implicit unrealistic and counterproductive assumption in the current WTO regime: once liberalised, industries should remain open forever. Interestingly, each WTO member does not follow this assumption in its own domestic affairs: it recognises the need for 'recontracting' the commitments that are the basis of the free trade regime between its various regions, and it uses a range of different instruments in this respect flexible local regulations (federal regime), public investment, subsidies of all kinds, etc.

Such a realistic approach should be extended to the GATT-WTO regime, which is now robust enough to adopt it. In the international trade system, there is one key instrument available for recontracting: renegotiating existing commitments under GATT Article XXVIII (for goods) and GATS Article XXI (for services). Currently, trade remedies are implicitly used as unilateral recontracting of the commitments of the countries implementing them—making them an implicit substitute for GATT-GATS renegotiation provisions. In fact, the use of the GATT renegotiation procedure declined in the early 1980s, precisely at the time when anti-dumping procedures were increasingly being used.

Renegotiating commitments should therefore be recognised as the ultimate trade remedy. However, making renegotiation the strategic pillar for addressing the problem of trade remedies raises three practical problems. If trade remedies are necessary only for a limited period, renegotiation looks a 'disproportionate' instrument. Trade remedies should be available rapidly, whereas renegotiations require time. Too many and frequent renegotiations might blur the long-term movement towards liberalisation to a dangerous extent.

There is therefore a need to limit the frequency of renegotiations, hence the following proposal: trade remedies would continue to exist, but all would be 'locked' by the renegotiation process so that they could be used for only a limited period. In other words, a WTO member would not be allowed to escape for 'too long' its commitments through trade remedies: after a predetermined period, it would be forced either to eliminate its 'transitory' reprotection or to renegotiate its existing commitments.

Such an approach has several decisive advantages in the long run. First, by putting renegotiations as the direct source of disciplines on WTO trade remedies, it relies on the most powerful discipline possible in the WTO forum. Also, it does not require an (impossible) rewriting of the existing GATT-GATS texts: rather, it makes full use of them by combining them in the most logical way (instead of leaving them side by side). Third, this approach can easily be applied to services, where trade remedies are likely to play an even more important role for several reasons: existing instruments of protection can rarely be fine-tuned (unlike tariffs); their values as concessions are almost impossible to compute; and their expected impact is very hard to assess. All these features will make the liberalisation process less incremental to implement and more difficult to control in services than in goods. By the same token, they make the combination of transitory trade remedies (GATS X) and renegotiation (GATS XXI) an argument even more compelling in services than in goods.

This approach has also advantages in the short to medium term. It would be a strong force in favour of a progressive shift towards one trade remedy: safeguards. Being substitutable, the many trade remedies currently available compete between themselves to provide relief (de jure) and permanent protection (de facto). The success of anti-dumping comes from the fact that it guarantees the best deal (the highest level of protection) for complainants and hence the greatest damage to existing WTO commitments. Almost all empirical economic studies, including those from agencies involved in anti-dumping procedures show that the vast majority of anti-dumping cases are driven by the will to provide protection to industries claiming to be in trouble: less than 10 per cent of EU and US anti-dumping cases would have a chance to succeed without arguments associated with protection, as shown by Morkre and Kelly, Finger, Greenaway, Shin, Bourgeois and Messerlin and Winters.

To sum up, the world trade regime of the early 2000s is robust enough to recognise the need for recontracting in some circumstances. All the trade remedies should be subjected to the same discipline: being transitory and, at the end of the transition period, being locked by the choice between elimination or renegotiation of the corresponding commitments. Moreover, there should be a progressive shift from the existing trade remedies to an unified safeguard procedure and a shift from trade remedy to competition law for the tiny portion of cases raising competition issues (less than 10 per cent in the case of anti-dumping).

Progressive Implementation

The most difficult task will be to implement the above principles progressively. This section aims at sketching a minimal programme of reforms. In this respect, the opposition (from the US government) to official negotiations on such issues for the coming round is not such a severe obstacle because a lot of the work could be initiated in the ad hoc WTO committees, so that once enough material has been accumulated, it could be shifted to a full negotiating working group. However, these ad hoc committees should meet in joint sessions in order to ensure that potential reforms in one trade remedy are not ruined by the absence of reforms in other trade remedies (since all are substitutable). A minimal programme should include three sources of improvement.

Anchoring safeguards to renegotiation

GATT XIX on safeguards has been largely unused precisely because it was not a back door to protection as 'efficient' as GATT-illegal VERs (during the 1970s) or as anti-dumping procedures (since the 1980s). The reasons for its relative 'inefficiency' are well known: strictly non-discriminatory and transitory measures; a high risk of retaliation by trading partners; and the fundamental recognition that the protection to be granted flows from the failure of the domestic industry. All these features are in sharp contrast to anti-dumping measures, which allow almost unlimited discrimination for unlimited periods, which run almost no risk of retaliation, which are based on the assertion that the protection to be granted is caused by 'unfair' foreign behaviour, and which ignore the need for 'adjustment'.

The Uruguay Round Safeguard Agreement has been a notable effort to 'revitalise' the safeguard instrument while trying to maintain intact its key positive features. On balance, it has brought net benefits, and it constitutes a valuable basis on which to build additional progress (it is consistent with the strategic choices described above). It has introduced two essential improvements: a clarification of the notion of transitory measures (for a period of four years, renewable once), and the elimination of all VERs and other 'grey' measures (although effective elimination may have been notably related to substituted anti-dumping measures). The silence of the Safeguard Agreement on the 'ongoing liberalisation' and 'unforeseen development' conditions included in GATT XIX are rather positive: it has made safeguard a possible competitor to anti-dumping, not only for the limited period of ongoing liberalisation but also in much wider circumstances. This is a reasonable move if one accepts the notion that recontracting is a 'natural' phenomenon, and a necessary move if one wants a progressive elimination of anti-dumping. The only real cost of the Uruguay Round Safeguard Agreement has been to allow a more discriminatory use of quotas.

An improved Safeguard Agreement should make more robust the concept of transitory protection. It should specify that, at the end of the second period of enforcing safeguard measures, the country will have the choice between only two alternatives: to renegotiate the tariffs on the goods subject to safeguard measures, or to eliminate these measures. In the latter case, shifting to other trade remedies should be prohibited a first recognition of the fact that all trade remedies should converge to a single type. Lastly, the two transition periods of safeguards should be reduced from four to three years in order to fit explicitly with the renegotiation procedure under GATT XXVIII.

Disciplining Anti-Dumping Reviews

Anti-dumping reviews represent the strongest systemic threat to the WTO regime because they perpetuate what was meant to be transitory protection. Reviews leading to renewed anti-dumping measures would make sense in only two situations. import-competing firms aim at perpetuating reprotection; and alleged dumpers and import-competing firms aim at implementing long-term VER-type deals under anti-dumping regulations. Both situations have little to do with alleged anti-dumping logic but a lot to do with protection.

Introducing more disciplines in anti-dumping reviews should be a priority. There is a wide spectrum of possible reforms. The minimum effort would consist of closing all existing procedural loopholes, such as the obligation (weaker for reviews than for initial cases) to compare domestic and foreign prices on an average-to-average or transaction-to-transaction basis. A bolder approach would consist of introducing all the improvements of substance that are suggested below in the reviews making disciplines in reviews a test for disciplines to be introduced later in initial anti-dumping cases. The boldest reform would be to eliminate anti-dumping reviews completely and replace them with safeguards (in turn, this would require limiting the time frame of the initial anti-dumping cases to three years): this shift is the logical consequence of the absence of an anti-dumping rationale in the case of reviews (as mentioned above), and it corresponds to another step towards a single trade remedy.

Reducing the current biases in favour of dumping determination

Finding dumping is the key step in anti-dumping cases: it comes first in the investigation procedure (hence it heavily determines the next stages), and it is potentially the most 'objective' to the extent that, compared with subsequent stages (injury determination and causal relationship), it relies more on facts. Focusing on dumping determination is also justified, because dumping margins have shown a tendency to increase, which underlines the urgent need for improved disciplines.

A minimal programme could include several 'minimal' reforms. First, the exceptions to the requirement that price comparison should be average-to-average or transaction-to-transaction (an almost certain recipe for finding dumping) should be eliminated. Second, existing biases in the definition of foreign normal value should be reduced. For instance, when there are no (or negligible) domestic sales but when there are export sales, export prices should be considered the mandatory source of information. The exclusion of an exporter's home-market sales at a loss from 'actual data' (through the notion of 'ordinary' course of trade, which is a systematic way of inflating constructed values) should be eliminated. Third, the period to be taken into account by the investigation should be extended, a reform essential in anti-dumping cases dealing with cyclical activity (an important source of anti-dumping activity in developing countries). It is possible to have a sense of the potential impact of certain reforms. For instance, out of the 208 EU and US anti-dumping cases initiated between 1995 and 1998 (with the necessary information), only thirteen (6 per cent) have been based exclusively on a direct price comparison, and there is a (monotonously) increasing average margin of dumping when one departs from price comparison from 3 to 95 per cent in the USA and from 22 to 74 per cent in the EU.

Two additional reforms not directly related to dumping determination could be envisaged. First, it would be important to reduce (preferably eliminate) the possibility of accumulating allegedly 'dumped' imports over countries. Prusa has provided evidence that mandatory accumulation in the US regulations has caused an extra 100 cases to be filed between 1984 and 1994, but it has also changed the ITC's determination in about sixty cases (all other things being constant). Similar results have been found for the EU. A weaker variant would be to ban accumulation of imports from countries representing less than a given percentage of total imports. For instance, WTO members could agree to start from a low threshold and increase it during the enforcement period of the coming round, or they could agree to increase it in the negotiations of future rounds (a first example of a 'threshold-based' approach, see below). The other additional reform would consist of prohibiting the initiation of anti-dumping cases if the allegedly dumped imports are already subject to quantitative restrictions, price surveillance or any other severe constraints on trade (such as public procurement representing a substantial portion of the market), which could be put on a list to be agreed on by WTO members. In other words, accumulating trade remedies is not acceptable a prohibition consistent with the long-term strategic choice of a unique trade remedy.

This minimal programme deserves a final remark. Because anti-dumping and safeguards are substitutable and competing, reforming safeguards and anti-dumping has to be conducted in parallel. All the above reforms for anti-dumping should therefore be introduced in safeguards (and vice versa). They could be introduced in similar terms when the two procedures are very similar (such as the definitions of the like-product or of the domestic industry). Or they could be introduced under a stronger form if required by the specifics of safeguards. For instance, the 'unforeseen development' condition could suggest that the de minimis share condition allowing small imports to be put out of anti-dumping reach could be higher in the case of safeguards (hence mirroring the fact that the development has to be unforeseen).

Progressive implementation: a more ambitious programme

Even if fully successful, the above minimal programme has no chance in the long term of curbing the number of anti-dumping cases and the derived protectionist drift. Sooner or later, all reforms of the anti-dumping component will be eroded or circumvented by complainants using the opportunity of new cases.

More ambitious reforms require the support of economic analysis. Economic issues associated with anti-dumping enforcement are related to price discrimination, cyclical dumping, and predatory and strategic pricing. Substantive reforms in anti-dumping should therefore reflect the economic analysis of these four issues. In a nutshell, this means that the new anti-dumping agreement should contain provisions making it difficult or impossible to open anti-dumping cases related to price discrimination and cyclical dumping, whereas it should prepare for the handling (probably in the distant future) of the very few predatory and strategic dumping cases by competition authorities under national competition laws. Ultimately, substantive reforms in anti-dumping should lead to the elimination of anti-dumping regulations and a progressive reallocation of existing anti-dumping cases into a red box (no economic or political justification), an orange box (no economic justification, but political constraints requiring the use of safeguards), and a green box (economic justification requiring the use of competition law).

This process could be eased substantially by using an approach based on negotiated quantitative 'thresholds'. A threshold-based approach has three key advantages: it is easily negotiable (negotiators can talk in terms of figures or percentages); it gives a sense of the magnitude of the concessions granted by both sides; and it can be tightened (through more binding thresholds) in future rounds hence it can deliver the progressive liberalisation that WTO members are looking for. Moreover, it can be used in trade-offs, including issues other than anti-dumping or trade remedies: for instance, heavy users of anti-dumping measures could trade stricter reforms in anti-dumping in exchange for better access to foreign markets in goods or services.

Limiting the number of anti-dumping complaints

Anti-dumping complaints depend upon three key definitions: a major proportion of the industry, de minimis conditions, and like-product. Complaining firms should constitute the major proportion of the domestic industry. 'Domestic' firms and the 'major proportion' have no unequivocal definitions. For instance, requiring that complaining firms represent a large (25 to 50 per cent) aggregate market share may minimise the number of potential complainants, but it implies that potential oligopolies or monopolies can complain more easily than the many firms in a competitive environment. And it does not exclude a small firm if the definition of the product is narrow enough. Rather, what counts is the aggregate market share of the complainants and defendants (and its breakdown by firm), because this information will reveal the risks of making the investigated market less competitive by imposing anti-dumping measures (as a reminder, complainants and defendants having a combined market share larger than 95 per cent represent almost a third of the total number of EU and US cases). Asking for public information on the market shares of all major firms involved in the anti-dumping proceedings looks to be a minimal requirement. A stronger variant would be to prohibit the initiation of anti-dumping cases with an aggregate (complainants and defendants) market share above a given threshold. This threshold could be tightened up progressively an illustration of the 'threshold-based' approach suggested above.

Anti-dumping cases with 'negligible imports' (3 per cent of total imports on an allegedly dumping country basis, with a collective cap of 7 per cent for all the countries involved) are not permitted under current anti-dumping regulations. However, this de minimis provision makes little sense (particularly, in terms of predatory and strategic pricing), because it refers to import shares: market shares should be defined in terms of domestic consumption in the importing country. Agreeing on a de minimis threshold of 5 per cent of domestic consumption would be a relatively conservative decision and WTO members could agree to increase this threshold during the implementation phase of the round (or to negotiate further increases during subsequent rounds).

Anti-dumping investigations start by defining whether domestic and foreign products are like-products. In economic terms, like-products are defined in terms of substitution (the magnitude of their price cross-elasticities determines the 'relevant' market). This market-based definition has already surfaced in a few dispute settlement cases, when the like-product definition has been linked to 'competition in the marketplace'. However, it would be difficult to extend this link to anti-dumping in general because of the absence of robust legal ground and because the benefits of such an extension on the number and outcome of anti-dumping cases are far from clear.

Rather, an acceptable reform could consist of simply imposing transparency in these matters: a list of the like-products tabled by the complainants/defendants but excluded by the investigating authorities, and a detailed description of the markets and of the firms operating in them (firms' market shares, and connections between firms, if any). Such transparency would almost provide the information necessary for a preliminary assessment of the relevant market in a typical competition case, but without requiring the complex and sophisticated procedures of competition cases.

Injury determination

Existing anti-dumping regulations have no clear methodology when estimating injury: what counts today is less a matter of economic assessment than of political opportunity and clout. The existing criteria for injury determination are potentially redundant (relative price changes can explain market share changes, and vice versa), and they can reflect quite healthy evolutions (a declining market share of a domestic monopoly or dominant firm is the healthy outcome of competition).

Ideally, reforms should aim at making a distinction between competitive trade shocks (healthy because they provide benefit to domestic users, even if they require adjustment from inefficient domestic producers) and competition 'distorted' by the strategic behaviour of foreign firms (based on predation or on the existence of a protected 'sanctuary' market in the exporting country). The best compromise between the existing legal framework and minimal economic analysis is the use of partial equilibrium models, allowing the estimation of firms' revenue losses related to dumping (and the benefits for users), all other things being constant. The simple criterion of revenue losses could be privileged. The use of such models could be made mandatory, or it could merely be seen as a systematic source of information. In both cases, the model used and the estimates obtained by the model should be published in the official anti-dumping proceedings of each case in order to fulfil the transparency objective.

If WTO members are sufficiently reform-minded, they could introduce thresholds in the use of partial equilibrium models. For instance, no measure should be imposed in cases where the level of injury losses is less than an agreed threshold (x per cent) of the revenues of the initial year a threshold that could be increased later by new negotiations (as a reminder, complainants with losses larger than 5 per cent of their 'pre-dumping' revenues represent only one-third of the total number of EU and US anti-dumping cases, including those dealing with non-competitive market structures.

It is essential to make parallel reforms in anti-dumping and safeguard. As is well known, GATT XIX refers to serious injury (as opposed to material injury in anti-dumping). The specific definition of serious injury could be reflected by a slightly different threshold for revenue losses than for material injury: for instance, material injury would occur when the losses of domestic firms were larger than 10 per cent of their revenues, whereas serious injury could be said to occur when their losses were larger than 15 or 20 per cent (possibly to be strengthened in future negotiations).

Anti-dumping and safeguard measures

A substantial proportion of anti-dumping measures do not consist of duties but of price or quantity undertakings (underlining the safeguard nature of anti-dumping). Re-establishing the pre-eminence of tariffs, which do not generate those private rents capable of fuelling long-term protection (in particular, when shared between foreign and domestic firms) seems essential.

Banning anti-dumping measures other than duties could be envisaged. However, it may run the risk of triggering private rent-sharing agreements before the official termination of the case. Such a risk could be managed to a certain extent by requiring a stricter and more complete notification procedure of the anti-dumping cases not terminated by anti-dumping duties, and by imposing a cross-examination of these cases by the WTO Safeguard Committee after three years in order to check for the absence of any 'grey' measure. But there is a better alternative to such a ban: that anti-dumping investigations not terminated by tariffs should not be subject to anti-dumping reviews, or that they could be prolonged only under the same conditions as those imposed on safeguards during their second period of enforcement (again implying that they could last only three years).

Measures are where anti-dumping and safeguards differ the most: anti-dumping allows for endlessly discriminatory measures, whereas sticking to GATT XIX would impose non-discriminatory measures a sure recipe for maintaining the current primacy of anti-dumping for ever. Among the many possible reforms, the most logical would be to limit the non-discriminatory requirement on safeguards to initial negotiators or principal countries. It maintains the non-discrimination discipline for the major existing competitors (it opens the door to discrimination only in favour of emerging competitors. It substantially reduces the gap between anti-dumping and safeguards, because anti-dumping tends de facto to target all the major competing countries (the gap remains unaltered to the extent that anti-dumping can impose different measures on different firms from every trading partner). Lastly, it has a legal logic: renegotiation (one of the two possible ultimate results of a safeguard action) is subject to a provision of the same nature.

The 'national interest' clause allows a WTO member that has demonstrated the existence of dumping and injury not to take protectionist measures on the grounds that such measures would harm other parts of the domestic economy. In other words, this clause opens the door to the introduction of domestic consumers' interests, which so far have been excluded from the anti-dumping procedure. As mentioned above, this clause has not worked well: it comes too late in the procedure, at a time when it is very hard for the authorities to say 'no' to the complaining firms requesting protection.

Many reforms proposed above (in particular, those about more information and transparency) will de facto reinforce the national interest clause. One could add a last reform with a systemic dimension: each WTO member that has enforced more than a given number of anti-dumping actions during a defined period would be required to provide an economic report on all the cases investigated for the WTO Council. Ideally, these reports (due, say, every three years) should include an assessment of the estimated costs of the anti-dumping measures adopted during the period and an analysis of the impact of the measures on the domestic market structure. These reports would constitute the economic basis for a pluri-annual review of anti-dumping practices to be done within the WTO and, hopefully, the basis for future reforms.

Summary

There is no anti-dumping provision in the GATS and following the disastrous experience of anti-dumping in goods one can only hope that there never will be. But there is an embryonic safeguard clause: GATS Article X on 'emergency safeguard measures' merely states that 'there shall be multilateral negotiations on the question of emergency safeguard measures', and that future GATS X shall be 'based on the principle of non-discrimination'.

WTO members should not miss the unique opportunity to create a safeguard regime for services parallel to what should ideally exist in goods: locking the use of GATS X with GATS XXI (renegotiations), making transitory safeguard measures under GATS X (with only one renewal) possible. Most of the detailed provisions (like-services, a major proportion of the industry, etc.) do not raise specific issues for services, at least conceptually (enforcement may be more difficult).

However, safeguards in services raise two specific problems. The first is the 'cross-modality' of GATS X: should emergency safeguard measures be defined by mode of delivery, or not? The economically sound answer is that GATS X should be 'cross-modal', that is, enforced across all modes. Like the need to define de minimis shares in terms of domestic consumption, any 'surge' in service imports should be judged on the basis of the domestic consumption of the service in question (independently of the mode of delivery): what counts is the domestic situation, not the fact that 'disturbances' have been created by imports, the movements of consumers or producers, or commercial presence.

The second problem is as follows: could safeguard measures take all the possible forms (including quantitative restrictions), or should they be limited to certain forms (ad valorem tariffs). Some caution seems necessary here. In particular, quantitative restrictions may deserve a fresh look in the case of services: although they are likely to have the same downsides in services as in goods (opaqueness, rents creating permanent vested interests, a capacity to isolate the domestic market from world markets, etc.), they may have 'good' sides (relative to other instruments) because they may be easier to enforce in a non-discriminatory way and to monitor in a transparent manner.

The last comment is that this paper has adopted a very pragmatic tone. It should be made clear that, from the economist's perspective, the best proposals are the most radical or alternatively that any departure from the maximum programme will have a price to pay in domestic and world inefficiencies and/or conflicts. The economist's stance flows from the fact that, although it is always possible to find cases where, at least in theory, anti-dumping might not be welfare-deteriorating, a careful study of existing cases suggests a quite different story.

10

Metamorphosing the World Trade Organization

Introduction

International trade was conducted primarily through trading blocs among countries with similar economic systems and complementary needs. There was no true "global" trade. In their zeal to compete, these blocs eventually became military blocs, and World War II began. After the war, international trade continued to be compartmentalized. There was no central authority and no agreed-upon or enforceable rules. The Bretton Woods/GATT conference was supposed to provide such a mechanism-the International Trade Organization (ITO). But the U.S. Congress opposed the ITO, because it didn't want America's trade practices policed by others. The U.S. wanted to do the policing and so the ITO never was created. In its place was the General Agreement on Tariffs and Trade, known as the GATT. But the GATT had no enforcement power and was never meant to be as far-reaching as it became by the end of the Uruguay Round.

The trading rules of the GATT are negotiated in sessions called rounds. The first GATT round was concluded in 1947, involved 23 nations and covered about one-half of world trade in goods. The next round, in 1949, involved only thirteen nations. From then until 1964, there were periodic renegotiations of the GATT, involving anywhere from 26 to 38 nations. The latest GATT round (the Uruguay Round), the eighth overall, was concluded on December 15, 1993, and signed into force in March 1994. It involved 117 nations and took seven years to complete. Moreover, it did not address just tariff barriers (as past GATT agreements had) but added trade in services, intellectual property, textiles and agriculture.

The number of nations involved in this international agreement is surprising enough, but the amount of trade regulated by the GATT is truly astounding. The first GATT round dealt with goods worth approximately $10 billion, while the Uruguay Round involved almost $7 trillion. It was the most ambitious and created a new umbrella organization the World Trade Organization (WTO). The WTO was the most contentious issue of these negotiations and frequently threatened to stall the round. The reason for this was that the WTO would have a legal status and enforcement power that the GATT lacked. The "general agreement" was just that. It was not enforceable except for moral suasion. The WTO charter, however, established an international mechanism to enforce the GATT. However, the GATT and WTO are threatened by regional trading groups that are constantly forming and may set different and competing standards.

WTO Structure

The WTO 's highest authority is the Ministerial Conference. It is composed of one representative from each WTO member state. It meets at least once every two years and decides any number of issues under a growing list of multilateral trade agreements. However, the administrative work of the WTO (the bulk of its work) is performed by subsidiary bodies. Of these, the principal one is the General Council, which reports to the Ministerial Conference. The meetings of the General Council take two forms: the Dispute Settlement Body, which oversees the procedures for dispute settlement, and the Trade Policy Review Body, which conducts regular reviews of the trade policies of WTO member states.

WTO Decisions

The WTO tried to maintain the GATT tradition of consensus decision making. If a consensus cannot be reached, a vote is taken, but only in limited circumstances. Each country has one vote, but different decisions require varying majorities of the votes cast. The adoption of an interpretation of any of the multilateral trade agreements or a waiver of an obligation imposed on a member by a multilateral agreement requires a three-quarters majority. Amendments to the provisions of the multilateral agreements and the admission of a new member require a two-thirds majority.

In order to understand the importance of the WTO, the weakness of the GATT must be recalled. Under the GATT, a complaint by one member that another had engaged in unfair trade practices went through a process called "dispute resolution" or "dispute settlement." Their dispute was heard by a "panel" of three independent legal experts. The panel considered arguments from both sides and then issued a ruling. That ruling then had to be ratified by the GATT membership in order to become effective. Therein lay the problem. The offending nation could vote against implementation and block the panel's ruling. Although compliance often was achieved through political pressure, it was never consistent or assured. Many countries, including the U.S., simply ignored GATT rulings. The WTO charter avoided this problem by requiring only a consensus. In the WTO, however, the consensus must be to reject the decision of the panel (called a "negative consensus"). This is a drastic change from the GATT. The "negative consensus" effectively eliminates a veto by the offending nation.

The weakness of the dispute resolution process had become evident. Something had to be done to expedite the process and put some teeth into it. Since the U.S. was no longer able to dictate the terms of world trade, it was in its best interest to have the agreed upon terms of world trade enforced. The new dispute settlement procedure was the sort of policing system that the U.S. had vetoed during the first round of the GATT. Now, however, the U.S. needed an international enforcer.

One of the first complaints brought under the WTO was brought by the U.S., together with Ecuador, Guatemala, Honduras and Mexico. It involved the European Union's "banana import regime." The regime granted privileged access to the EU for bananas from African, Caribbean and Pacific (ACP) countries under the Lome Convention. ACP states had historic trade ties with EU states by virtue of being former colonies or dependencies. The complaint argued that the banana regime violated fair trading rules by unfairly discriminating against non-Lome producers. This case is a perfect example of the difference between the GATT system and the WTO. A complaint previously had been filed under the old GATT regarding the same regime. The GATT also had found that the EU's program violated GATT trading rules. But the GATT's weaker dispute settlement procedures allowed the EU to block any remedial action.

In June 1997, a WTO panel found against the EU with respect to part of the complaint and for it on another part. The ACP countries were covered by a waiver granted by the WTO in 1994 that allowed special conditions of trade with developing nations. The quota and licensing system developed under Lomé was aimed at helping their economies. That was not a problem. But the panel condemned the licensing procedure insofar as it established import quotas. Under the GATT, the EU was able to block enforcement. Under the WTO 's negative consensus, standard blockage was not possible.

One way to avoid a panel decision, or perhaps to mitigate its effect, is to appeal. And appeal the EU did. In September 1997, however, an appellate body affirmed the panel's finding that the banana regime violated WTO fair trade practices and would have to be dismantled. On October 16, 1997, the EU announced that it would abide by the decision, but set no date to comply. This brought immediate reaction from the U.S. and the other parties to the suit.

Under the WTO 's dispute settlement procedures, the losing party has a "reasonable period of time" to implement a panel decision. The reasonable period is determined by one of three methods: mutual agreement, arbitration or the dispute settlement body. When the parties to the banana litigation could not reach a mutual agreement, they requested that the time frame be fixed by binding arbitration. An arbitrator was appointed and the EU requested fifteen months to comply, arguing that dismantling its regime would be extremely difficult and time consuming since it involved treaties with many ACP nations. The U.S. and the other complainants argued that the EU should not be allowed so much time. After all, it had been apparent for some time that the EU practice violated GATT rules. The WTO appointed arbitrator disagreed, concluding that the difficulty of implementing the decision would require at least fifteen months. He therefore gave the EU until. January 1, 1999, to comply with the decision. But the EU gave no evidence that it intended to meet that deadline, and the U.S., upset by the delay, threatened retaliation. It seems like a small matter, but the banana case has proved to be a real test of the dispute settlement process, including the right of the injured state to retaliate under Article 22. So far, the WTO has been equal to the task. But the EU, having accepted its defeat, still did not meet its GATT obligation, and the U.S. has claimed the right to retaliate, possibly setting off a tit-for-tat trade war.

Dispute Settlement Process

The Uruguay Round dispute settlement process just described has 27 articles. The new procedure allows any member government to submit a WTO complaint against another, often at the request of a national business that feels that GATT terms have been violated. The first step in the process is to request consultations with the government whose trade practices allegedly violate GATT rules. The offending party often will seek to delay adjudication through the process of consultation, but the complaining government can insist that a dispute panel be appointed if the consultation does not resolve the situation within 60 days. Once that request is made, another series of time limits begin. The panel must be created within two months of the request and panel members must be appointed within 20 days thereafter. The panel then has six to nine months to investigate the case and make a decision. Meanwhile, the nations can and usually do continue their settlement negotiations. It often is in their best interests to reach a mutually acceptable resolution before the panel decides the case. At any time prior to the implementation of the panel's decision, the two parties can suspend or abandon their dispute or resolve it. About one-fourth of the complaints brought to the WTO have been settled without ever reaching a panel. Panel reports are called "interim" reports and must be finalized and made legally binding within 60 days of the date of decision, unless either the losing party files a notice of appeal or the WTO membership decides (by consensus) not to finalize the report panel decision.

Appeals Process

Article 17 allows the losing party to appeal to an "Appellate Body." Of the panel reports circulated between 1995 and 1997 all were appealed. The reason for this is that the loser at the panel level almost always improves its position on appeal. Whereas the panel reaches a largely legal decision, the Appeal Body mixes in some policy as well. Besides, an appeal delays the enforcement of an adverse decision.

The Appellate Body has 60 days to rule on any claim of legal error. Its decision will become legally binding within 30 days, unless (again) the WTO membership decides by consensus not to finalize the decision. Overall, the WTO dispute settlement procedure has proven to be very effective, especially for the U.S. It has been the complainant in 39 of the first 114 complaints filled with the WTO. The EU also has been very active, having filed 25 complaints. The U.S. and the EU also have been named as defendants in more cases than any other WTO members, with the U.S. appearing as defendant in 26 and the European Union in 29. It appears from the number of cases brought by the U.S. compared to complaints brought against it that we benefit from the WTO mechanism, because enforcement would be quite difficult outside the WTO.

Enforcement of Decisions

Enforcement is possibly the most complex reform of the GATT system resulting from the Uruguay Round. Articles 21 and 22 establish a sequence of enforcement steps. The first is to decide how much time an offending nation has to comply with an adverse ruling. The standard period is fifteen months, but its length can vary with the situation. If compliance does not occur within the time allowed, the offending nation is given an additional 20 days to negotiate a reduction of the trade barriers in question or to set a reasonable compensation for the damage done. If these negotiations aren't successful, then the complaining nation is free to retaliate by setting trade barriers of its own against the offending nation. Should the offending nation feel that the retaliatory measures are excessive, then the two nations enter a binding arbitration procedure. Article 22:3 of the Uruguay Round agreement prohibits "cross retaliation." That occurs when the complaining nation imposes trade barriers against exports not the subject of the original suit. The new dispute settlement procedure established under the WTO applies to all the trading agreements contained in the final acts of the Uruguay Round.

As the number of nations and trade sectors covered by GATT increase, more and more complaints arise. Presently 134 nations and customs territories are members of the WTO. From its inception in 1994 to the end of 1997, 114 dispute settlement complaints were filed. The U.S. has used the dispute settlement procedure liberally. The ability to prosecute its trade grievances, even at the expense of being prosecuted, is the reason the U.S. finally favored the creation of the WTO.

The fact that the United States has used the WTO to resolve trade issues rather than resorting to unilateral means is not surprising, insofar as the WTO charter specifically states that WTO mechanisms shall be the only means of settling disputes between its members, under the covered agreements. The WTO proscribes unilateral responses to alleged trade violations. As a result, unilateral imposition of economic sanctions by one country against its trading partner should be ended. However, the dispute resolution mechanism permits the imposition of sanctions for continued violation of the agreements.

One example of such unilateral procedures is the Special 301 provisions under the U.S. Omnibus Trade and Competition Act of 1988. Special 301 is meant to deal exclusively with intellectual property. Within 30 days after the issuance of the National Trade Estimate Report, Special 301 directs the U.S. Trade Representative (USTR) to identify foreign nations whose trade practices are found to violate intellectual property rights. Those nations whose practices are particularly egregious are placed on a "priority watch list." Thirty days after that, the USTR must begin investigating the alleged illegal practices. If those practices do not abate within six months, the USTR is authorized (but not required) to retaliate by imposing import restrictions. However, Special 301 sanctions could violate the GATT by using unilateral measures. Using multilateral dispute settlement procedures is a better course of action.

U.S. Experience with the WTO

One of the first cases brought under the WTO's new procedures was against the U.S. In December 1994, Brazil and Venezuela complained that U.S. Environmental Protection Agency (EPA) rules for reformulated gasoline violated the GATT. Under the EPA's Clean Air Act, domestic refiners were allowed to set a baseline using the average quality of gasoline sold in 1990. The rule required foreign refiners to meet a different baseline. The EPA reasoned that this was necessary because foreign companies did not have complete data sets allowing them to set an accurate 1990 baseline. In January 1996, the first WTO dispute resolution panel decision found that the EPA provisions violated the GATT, and the U.S. could no longer set different baselines for foreign refiners. The U.S. appealed the panel's finding, but the decision was upheld. Having lost its appeal, the U.S. agreed to abide by the decision, setting June 1997 as the date. By January 1997 the U.S. still had not implemented changes, and Venezuela and Brazil complained that the U.S. delay "imposed costs on Brazilian gas exports on a daily basis." In February the U.S. announced it was on track to comply with the WTO ruling, and a mid-August 1997 deadline was set. On August 19, 1997, the U.S. finally adopted a rule granting foreign oil refineries the option to request fuel quality standards similar to those used at U.S. refineries.

Even though the first decision under the WTO regime went against the U.S., we continued our support. In order to assure enforcement of GATT rules we needed an international enforcement mechanism. The U.S. expected that it would profit more from the ability to enforce trading rules against our trading partners than they would in applying them to us. The U.S. has used the WTO dispute resolution process frequently, and it has been used almost as often against us. But the U.S. has won more cases than it has lost. Excepting the Venezuelan oil and Fuji film cases, the first few years of U.S. experience with the WTO has been reasonably positive.

One of those first winning cases involved hormone-fed U.S. beef. Since 1989, the EU has banned the import of U.S. beef produced by using synthetic growth hormones. The U.S. viewed this as a discriminatory practice, outlawed by the GATT, and accused the EU of using it to protect its own beef industry. The U.S. estimated that the ban prevented $250 million worth of beef exports to the EU annually. A WTO panel sided with the U.S., saying that the EU exclusion was "inconsistent with the requirements of the WTO 's agreement on the Application of Sanitary Phytosanitary Measures (SPS) because it was not based on a risk assessment of the potential adverse impact on human health." The EU appealed, and the appellate body reversed or modified several of the panel's conclusions. This is not an uncommon phenomenon, but the appeal decision only allowed the EU a second opportunity to prove that there was a health reason to exclude hormone-fed U.S. beef from the EU. It was in the EU's best interest to challenge the finding of the panel, and the appellate body did find that WTO members are entitled to a level of protection higher than current international standards. However, the appellate body agreed with the panel's finding that the EU had not scientifically justified its ban.

The appellate decision caused a stir because the standard for health protection previously had been an international standard. Now a WTO standard may be in the offing. The appellate body also overturned the panel with regard to the scope of risk assessments used to exclude on imported food for health reasons. Prior to the appellate body's decision, the standard was limited to laboratory methods commonly associated with the physical sciences. The appellate body allowed, however, that risk assessment could involve "risk in human societies as they actually exist, in other words, the actual potential for adverse effects to human health in the real world where people live and work and die." This makes the analytical process more subjective and places a shadow of uncertainty over other health-based import exclusions, such as the Canadian-Australian dispute about salmon imports or the U.S.-Japanese dispute regarding quarantine rules.

The EU used a "zero-risk" standard for imported beef. The irony is that the U.S. used that same "zero-risk" standard against the importation of EU beef. So the U.S. victory over the EU may cause it to reduce its own protections. Meanwhile, the WTO upheld the panel's decision, and the EU expressed its determination to keep the ban in place while it searched for further evidence of the dangers of hormone-fed beef. Eventually, a WTO appellate panel (in an unrelated case) declared that the risk assessment needed to check the spread of pests and disease is more stringent than that applied to threats to human and animal health posed by additives, but the latter must be ascertainable, not theoretical.

The debate over hormone-treated beef is not an isolated matter. It is closely intertwined with the importation of all foreign food. The EU wants a special labeling requirement for genetically modified food. Its labeling campaign is vigorously opposed by the U.S. as a protectionist measure. The U.S. estimates that the EU's labeling requirements would add approximately $5 billion in overhead to our agricultural exports. A number of disputes, such as the U.S. complaint about Japan's quarantine rules for imported fruits and vegetables, could be affected by the WTO 's resolution of the beef conflict.

One dispute that seemed to end in a draw involved photographic film. The complaint was promoted by the Eastman Kodak Co. It alleged that the Japanese government used a retail system that burdened foreign film in order to buffer Japanese market openings. Although, the case was technically between the U.S. and Japan, it began as a Section 301 trade case brought by Kodak, alleging violations of GATT rules. The complaint evolved into a WTO dispute between the U.S. and Japan, as each country took up the cause of its national "hero." The petition alleged that the Japanese government systematically created barriers to the sale of imported consumer photographic paper and film by allowing domestic film makers to control wholesale film distribution. Fuji was the alleged beneficiary of these government actions. In September 1995, a WTO panel was formed to decide whether Japan had violated GATT rules, using non-tariff barriers. One year later, the dispute settlement panel rejected the U.S. claim. This was not the end of the dispute, however. In February 1998, the USTR announced that she would form an "interagency monitoring and enforcement committee" to test the validity of Japan's claim that it had an open film market. So the WTO process is not always the end of the matter.

It is less the content than the context of these disputes that matters to the WTO members. Just about every nation that has commented on the WTO 's dispute settlement body (DSB) procedures (currently under review) agrees they are too slow. Moreover, they are legal only at that trial level and are influenced by political considerations on appeal. American representatives are frustrated when they lose what they consider strong cases or wait seemingly forever for enforcement when vindicated (bananas; beef hormones). Nonetheless, the U.S. and the EU have been pushing the envelope to its limits in the banana dispute. The condemned practice was not a simple piece of national legislation, but a multiparty agreement. Negotiations were delicate. Moreover, the U.S. was pushing for a prompt dispute panel review of the EU's substituted program and threatened unilateral sanctions if the dispute dragged on. It was all very new (and politically charged) terrain for the WTO and its members.

The U.S. behavior might be justified if the U.S. had not done very well in the dispute settlement process. But why put so much pressure on the system that it might collapse? The U.S. has not made any friends among those WTO members (including its litigation partners and the EU) who know that the process is partly political and that trade agreements must be given time to mature and strengthen. In due course the banana dispute is likely to be resolved. Moreover, the EU already has agreed to allow the import of U.S. hormone-fed beef (another case they lost to the U.S. in the WTO). And the EU suspended (but did not drop) its complaint in the WTO that the Helms-Burton law (probably an illegal secondary boycott) violated the GATT. If other members can be sensitive to the pressures on the neophyle WTO, why cannot the U.S.? Perhaps the answer lies in a little-discussed provision of the U.S. legislation implementing the Uruguay Round that allows us to revoke U.S. membership in the WTO if it rules against the U.S. three times in five years. With two clear losses before the year 2000, perhaps U.S. litigators are playing to Congress, showing that the WTO works to our benefit. Indeed, it does. And it would be insane to walk away from so useful a vehicle when there is not an equal one in sight.

A full review of the WTO's dispute settlement system was well underway before these latest strains were placed up on it. Among common complaints are that it is slow, too secretive, and that outside parties – particularly nongovernmental organizations (NGOs) are not allowed to make input into or to observe the proceedings. Revisions are likely to speed up and strengthen the system and are likely to be adopted before the next round of trade negotiations.

Meanwhile, sectoral talks are continuing in a variety of areas. Some could bear fruit early in the new century. The financial services agreement reached in December 1997 was ratified by fewer than one-third of its 70 signatories by the agreed-upon deadline in early 1999, but ratifications continue. The agreement covers 95 percent of global financial services (bank lending, securities and insurance) worth $58 trillion. Fast action also is urged in the fields of agriculture and other services (although U.S./ EU bickering about the former has slowed progress in that area). Both topics were on the "built in" agenda for the GATT ministerial meeting held in November 1999 in the United States.

That meeting, among the last before a full GATT round begins again, served as a preview of what has been dubbed the "Millennium Round." The U.S. was lukewarm to the idea for the longest time, but support from other WTO members grew steadily. Eventually, in his 1999 State of the Union address, President Clinton endorsed the idea, calling for an "ambitious" round that would produce "concrete early results." He urged that intellectual property protection and government procurement be emphasized. Developing countries are accepting of the new round but want it to be limited. They fear that they will be forced by industrialized nations into tariff concessions that will threaten their economies. They also want to keep labor and environmental standards off the agenda.

The WTO also is under some pressure to expand its membership. Latvia's admission in February 1999 (only the second ex-Soviet member) brought membership to 134. But there are some 30 states on the waiting list, including China, Russia and Taiwan. The former two are particularly anxious to join, but their accession presents a classic dilemma in "globalization." The WTO should be as inclusive as possible, but it should set a single, high standard. It may be easier to work with countries that are members, but once they achieve that goal the greatest reason to liberalize their economies disappears. So accession negotiations are typically difficult. China was dedicated to becoming a member by the year 2000, in time for the "Millennium Round." That put immense pressure on its government to make trade concessions. But there also is pressure on the WTO to compromise, and let the world's most populous nation in. Russia's prospects are not nearly so good.

Side Agreements and Sectoral Agreements

Side agreements are sub-agreements to the GATT, to which not all members of the Uruguay Round are party. However, they were negotiated during a full GATT round. These appear in Annex 4 to the Treaty, which lists all side agreements. They deal with such diverse subjects as civilian aircraft, government procurement, dairy products and bovine meat. They bind only those GATT members that are signatories.

Like side agreements, sectoral agreements are binding only on those individual WTO members that voluntarily subscribe. But, unlike the side agreements, sectoral agreements are not concluded under a fall GATT round. The sectoral agreements often deal with issues that could not be concluded during a regular round, for fear of stalling the process. As a result, these agreements are negotiated separately, outside the GATT. Because it takes so long to negotiate a full GATT round, sectoral agreements became the preferred form of multilateral trade agreement in the late 1990s. The reason is that they permitted focused negotiation on a single area of trade, whereas a full round forces members to get involved in a much broader area of negotiation. Among the sectoral agreements currently being pursued are financial services, telecommunications and many more.

It seems foregone that there will be another GATT round, the Millennium Round, beginning in the year 2000. Even if a full round does begin, it may take years to complete. Meanwhile, sectoral agreements may be negotiated. Much has been accomplished through them, and while it is likely that a full round might eventually absorb them, they remain an important negotiating tool. For example, consider the information technology case, in the following section.

Information Technology

The sectoral agreement that has been the greatest success so far is the agreement on information technology (ITA). It was worked out at the WTO ministerial meeting in Singapore in 1996. The ITA committed signatories to the elimination of customs tariffs on computers, semiconductors and other products of information technology in July 1997. The agreement covers over 180 products, which are estimated to account for over $600 billion in sales annually. The agreement has been signed by some 45 countries, representing

93 percent of world trade in information technology, both goods and services. Talks continue about expanding the agreement to cover more products. These talks, dubbed ITA-II, involve the U.S., Australia, Canada, the EU, Hong Kong, Japan, New Zealand, Norway, Switzerland and Taiwan. What products will be covered by ITA-II is not clear, but it may add as many as 250 new products. The date set for reaching agreement was September 1998, but that date has slipped. Any further ITA opening is likely to be modest, because Asian economies in decline do not feel they can make trade concessions.

Telecommunications

Another sectoral agreement was concluded in the field of telecommunications. It contains commitments to open trade in the international supply of telecommunications equipment and services and allows foreign firms to establish a domestic presence and operate an independent telecommunication network as a competitor to local providers. The agreement opens up not only voice communications, but electronic data transmission as well. Sixty-nine countries signed the agreement. They account for more than 90 percent of telecommunication business, with annual revenue of $600 billion. Most signatory countries agreed that implementation should start in early 1998. However, the U.S. and Morocco were unwilling to do so. The U.S. did not want to be bound before knowing how things would work under the agreement in countries that had not yet ratified it. The Council agreed to extend the deadline until July 1998. The delay concerned some signatories, however, because the Fourth Protocol to the General Agreement on Trade in Services (GATS) states that, if not all members have signed by the deadline, those that have ratified may set a new date for the agreement to enter into force.

The European Commission has threatened to sue the U.S. for violations of the fourth protocol, which could be a harbinger of things to come. With telecommunications networks opening up worldwide, issues of interconnection and the fees to be charged foreign entrants will increase. There also are issues of the availability of radio frequencies (to accommodate mobile communications) and the use of differing satellite systems. Many problems remain to be worked out, but the belief is that the benefits of an agreement outweigh our present segmented system of telephony. It is believed that liberalization could be worth over $1 trillion in revenues by the year 2010.

Financial Services

Following closely on the heels of the telecommunications agreement came another sectoral agreement, this time dealing with financial services. The agreement is meant to open banking, insurance and securities markets to foreign competition in 95 percent of the global financial services market. It would cover financial services in 70 countries and commit another 50 to binding WTO rules, subject to dispute settlement procedures. The agreement encompasses $17.8 trillion in global securities assets, $38 trillion in global (domestic) bank lending and $2.2 trillion in worldwide insurance premiums. The final pact was agreed in December 1997 and was supposed to take effect in March 1999. Due to financial instability in Asia and worldwide, ratification has been slow.

Maritime

When the Uruguay Round of GATT was concluded in December 1994, three service areas upon which the negotiators could not agree (financial services, telecommunications and maritime transport) were taken off the table. Meanwhile, substantial sectorial progress has been made in the former two areas. But the shipping sector remains stuck in neutral. Up until mid1996, negotiations were ongoing in the WTO 's Maritime Committee. Of 37 participating nations, 24 had tabled offers to liberalize maritime trades. However, the U.S. refused to make any offer until its partners agreed to "approximate the current openness of the U.S. market." As the arbitrary deadline for agreement approached and other nations had not satisfied the U.S., its representatives walked away from the negotiations, saying that existing offers "merely sought to lock in place restrictive, and anticompetitive measures" in each country. Japan and the EU were eager to reopen the talks again in 1997 or 1998, but the U.S. was content to leave them "on hold" until the year 2000, when a new round of trade talks is likely to be launched.

Multilateral Agreement on Investment

A Multilateral Agreement on Investment (MAI) was negotiated by representatives of the 29 member countries of the OECD and a representative from the EU. The process, begun in 1995, is intended to commit nations to a policy of non-discrimination in the field of investments.

The OECD conducted the negotiations because many emerging nations were hesitant to liberalize their investment markets. Now the economic problems in Asia and the need of those nations for foreign investment means they will have to liberalize their financial markets and make them more transparent. So there is a push to move the MAI under the WTO umbrella. But before that, it had run into numerous snags. A group of 50 nongovernmental organizations (NGOS) vowed to campaign against the MAI unless it refocused negotiations to account for labor and the environment. Their concern is that the agreement would eventually "elevate the rights of investors far above those of workers, and [concern for] the environment." Then France walked out of the OECD talks, effectively shifting momentum to the WTO. It is unclear whether or not an MAI will ever be reached, but it is an important enough objective that negotiations are expected to continue. Indeed, the financial turmoil recently experienced makes an agreement more necessary.

State Aid

The Uruguay Round agreement required WTO members to substantially reduce state aid, particularly for agriculture. State aid is a government subsidy to a particular industry. This subsidizing usually is justified by the need to stabilize or preserve an industry, but in fact it distorts competition. The practice has been the topic of numerous WTO disputes; arising when an exporting country feels that it is put at a disadvantage when a national subsidy is given to domestic enterprises.

A typical form of state aid is that seen in Canada's dairy industry. Canada maintains a system of special milk classes through which it maintains high domestic prices. It also provides export subsidies for dairy products going into world markets. These subsidies are restricted by the GATT, but there are exceptions. New Zealand has complained that Canada is providing export subsidies for dairy products without regard to its WTO commitment. The U.S., Argentina and the EU have also joined in the informal consultations.

Procurement

During the Tokyo GATT Round, parties agreed that federal government purchasing would be governed by a procurement code, intended to open up government contracts to competitive bids and eliminate favoritism for national providers. However, the agreement was not signed by many countries, and those that did sign insisted upon sizable exceptions. Furthermore, subordinate governmental units (states, provinces and cities) are not covered. The U.S. wanted a better agreement. It especially wanted to compete for public procurement contracts of European sub-governmental units. Conversely, the EU wanted access to the public procurement market in the U.S. The result of this mutual interest was the Government Procurement Agreement (GPA) that became effective in January 1996. It provides for nondiscrimination and transparency with respect to government purchasing. Procurement decisions under the agreement are to be taken on the basis of economic considerations only. The GPA is a voluntary agreement and binds only those sub-units that agree. Thirty-seven of our 50 states have signed the agreement.

These cases demonstrate the difficulty of establishing simple, uniform and enforceable rules for international trade. Not only must divergent national interests and practices be harmonized, but semiautonomous governmental units must be brought aboard as well.

Origin

In July 1996, the U.S. implemented rules placing duties on textiles depending upon their country of origin. The EU then filed a complaint arguing that the new rules were obstacles to trade. U.S. rules of origin state that, for custom purposes, a textile product originates wherever the cloth was manufactured, not where it was cut or fabricated. Historically, rules of origin have been important because different tariffs or quotas apply depending on where a product "originates." Harmonization of rules of origin under the WTO has been slow and sketchy. Although it is progressing now, the original deadline for completing an agreement was not met.

Nonetheless, the WTO Rules of Origin Committee was able to endorse over 1,000 rules covering non-agricultural. They have not been able to agree on more controversial issues concerning the origin of textiles and agricultural products, however. The textile conflict between the U.S. and the EU is especially sharp.

In general, WTO rules provide that a product originates at the place of "substantial transformation." Textiles have been a problem since that sector was added to the GATT agenda in the Uruguay Round. The reason is that textiles (and agricultural products) often are the chief industries in emerging countries. It is natural for them to try to protect their domestic market from foreign competition and to penetrate foreign markets with inexpensive exports. The U.S. has been on both sides of the dispute regarding textiles. As complainant the U.S. filed a claim against Argentina and won, since Argentina's specific duties on textiles and apparel were excessive and violated WTO rules. The U.S. also has objected to the transshipment of Chinese textiles through Hong Kong to gain a lower tariff valuation.

Dumping

Harmonized rules also prohibit the dumping of products. In July 1997, South Korea filed a complaint against the U.S. in the WTO, alleging that it had levied unfair anti-dumping duties on Korean color television sets. The Antidumping Act of 1916 provides a remedy for dumping even in cases where predatory pricing is not alleged. The statute provides that importers are barred from selling articles in the U.S. at prices below actual market value in the country of production, if the importer intends to destroy, injure or prevent the establishment of a U.S. industry or to restrain or monopolize trade and commerce in the subject market. The act has been tested numerous times, but it has always survived. Although South Korea dropped its complaint regarding televisions, it continued to prosecute a suit objecting to dumping duties on dynamic random access memory semiconductors (DRAMs).

In January 1998, the WTO agreed to establish a panel to settle the dispute between the U.S. and South Korea over DRAMs. The panel will examine Korea's complaint that the U.S. anti-dumping duties are in violation of the WTO agreements, including the 1994 Anti-Dumping Agreement. Dumping complaints have increased with Asia's expansion, especially now that the region is trying to export its way out of its economic problems. But often such complaints are just another form of market protection.

Mutual Recognition

Mutual recognition is another GATT trade goal. The focus of mutual recognition treaties is to eliminate the cost of complying with different technical regulations and the certification process of different countries. Multiple inspections can slow trade and add to costs. Mutual recognition (where countries agree to recognize one another's testing and certification processes) eliminates these barriers. This does not mean a single standard for the whole world. Rather, it accepts that rigorous testing systems should produce results that need not be replicated. Obviously, this is a very lofty goal. But it is being realized, particularly in cutting-edge industries where standards evolve quite rapidly. WTO members are encouraged to enter into MRA negotiations with other members. The ISO 9000 standard series is an example of an international agreement leading to the establishment of an international standard. Mutual Recognition Agreements (MRAs) are increasingly made part of many technology agreements in both bilateral and multilateral settings.

Harmonization

Harmonization has been a goal of technical experts for many decades. The work of the International Standardization Organization (ISO) is instrumental in achieving that goal. Harmonization under the WTO also took a giant leap forward with the Technical Barriers to Trade agreement (TBT).

The agreement encourages WTO members to use existing international standards when formulating national ones. If this happens, over a period of time national (versus international) standards will gradually harmonize. Sometimes there is a good reason for differing national standards, however, as when national security is involved. However, the TBT agreement encourages members to join international bodies that will gradually harmonize national standards or set international ones.

The TBT recognizes the difficulties that developing nations face in meeting international technical standards. Therefore, it temporarily relaxes provisions that would require too rapid a change in standards. The TBT even allows for the preservation of indigenous technologies. The unique thing about harmonization, and a point often missed, is that it does not mean "the same" standards for all countries. Rather harmonization is the development of similar standards that do not pose obstacles to international trade.

Peripheral Agreements Insurance

Many sectoral agreements have sub-agreements, which may or may not have been fully negotiated when the sectoral agreements were concluded. One of these was the agreement on insurance, a part of the financial services agreement. This sub-agreement is aimed at opening up insurance markets to foreign companies. It covers the entire range of insurance products, including life, non-life, reinsurance, brokerage and auxiliary services. For U.S. companies in the insurance industry the agreement could expose a market worth more than $200 billion in foreign premiums. Fifty-two countries have joined the pact, guaranteeing broad market access, while another fourteen nations have committed to partially open their markets.

The U.S. put considerable pressure on India, Malaysia and Indonesia to open their health insurance markets. Enormous numbers of people who live in these countries have been unreachable by foreign insurance companies, because their national markets are completely closed. For a time it looked as if the negotiations would not be completed by the December 1997 deadline. In the end, the U.S. excluded Malaysia from the U.S. commitment. But many exemptions were granted at the last minute in order to get an agreement.

Labor

Once in a while GATT disputes arise that deal with human rights issues. Labor and human rights standards vary widely from developed to developing nations and yet they affect trade, for example, through the difference in the cost of goods produced by high-wage nations versus those produced by prison labor. Yet there are no well-defined GATT standards in the labor sector. Like the environment, the WTO finds itself in a very uncomfortable position. However, labor issues are starting to appear in WTO complaints and are testing the limits of the dispute resolution procedures. Like environmental issues, human rights issues are subjective and politically sensitive. The WTO cannot adjudicate them without adequate standards. Eventually, some international understanding must evolve. Thus far, the WTO has allowed the International Labor Organization (ILO) to take the lead.

Environmental

The WTO 's promotion of global trade also takes into account that increased trade can have a negative impact on the environment. However, former WTO Director General Ruggiero argued that trade liberalization can play an "important role" in protecting the environment by "reducing market inefficiencies." An agreement in the agricultural sector, for example, would help to reduce state subsidies to farmers and remove barriers to food imports. This is important because "study after study shows how market access restrictions, domestic support policies, and export subsidies have been the cause of direct and significant harm to the environment in many developed countries." They are concerned that the body, focused as it is on trade, will override national policies dealing with environmental protection. Several WTO decisions have done just this, finding that national environmental legislation violated the terms of the GATT. One WTO panel upheld Mexico's complaint that the U.S. dolphin-safe-tuna requirement was a violation of the international trade rules.

WTO rules provide that "governments can use any type of trade restriction, including import and export quotas and taxes for the purpose of environmental protection or resource protection as long as basic requirements relating to non-discrimination and least trade restrictiveness are met." Hence environmental-protection legislation is permissible as long as it is legitimate (not a subterfuge to protect domestic products) and does not materially interfere with the "process and production methods" of other traders. During the Uruguay Round, future WTO members agreed to examine ways to transfer environmental technology and services to developing countries, thereby improving their production processes environmentally. For the latter, the cost of this technology often is prohibitive.

However, environmental rules have been slow to develop in the WTO. This is partly because of their politically sensitive nature and partly because the issues are so complex. But the failure to lead has produced other concerns. Developed nations are concerned that the WTO will take the power to protect the environment out of the hands of individual nations, while developing nations are concerned that their economic growth will be slowed by the environmental legislation of developed nations.

One example of this tension is the so-called "shrimp/turtle" case. It involved the application of GATT rules to a trade dispute over the production and process methods (ppms) used when trawling for shrimp. Certain trawling methods allegedly kill sea turtles, a species that the U.S. considers endangered. The case involved competing trade and environment issues, each of which had merit. The WTO panel chose to seek advice from a group of environmental experts. This is the first time in WTO (or for that matter GATT) history that a dispute panel has formally sought outside expert advice.

The case turned on the panel's interpretation of Article XX of the GATT, which sets forth "General Exceptions" to GATT rules. In June 1987, the National Marine Fisheries Service enacted regulations requiring shrimp trawlers of a certain size operating in the Gulf of Mexico to use either turtle excluder devices (TEDS) or limit the time they tow shrimp nets without boarding a catch. A group of Louisiana shrimpers filed suit in federal court trying to block the regulation, but it was upheld. Of course, this put U.S. shrimpers at a disadvantage compared to non-Gulf fishermen, because it raised the cost of the catch (TED nets) or reduced their volume (shorter time). In November 1989, Congress passed legislation instructing the president to initiate negotiations to develop bilateral and multilateral agreements consistent with the national standard. The president delegated this duty to the State Department, which interpreted it as applying only to "the wider Caribbean and Western Atlantic region." This interpretation was challenged in the U.S. Court of International Trade, which found the regulation applied to "the importation of shrimp or products of shrimp wherever harvested." Thereafter, Thailand, Malaysia, India and Pakistan filed claims against the U.S. in the WTO.

Such cases are not new to the WTO. In fact, the shrimp-turtle case resembles the tuna-dolphin case decided under the GATT. The

U.S. tried to prohibit the importation of tuna from countries whose fishing fleets were not certified to be "dolphin safe." The dispute resolution panel found that the prohibition violated GATT rules, but the panel's ruling was never adopted because of the GATT's policy of consensus voting. One major difference between the tuna-dolphin case and the shrimp-turtle case, however, is that turtles have been recognized as being endangered by an international agreement.

In March 1998, the dispute settlement panel issued a preliminary ruling condemning the U.S. ban. The U.S. appealed the decision, believing that the ban was necessary to protect sea turtles from extinction and because Article XX allows exceptions to protect animal and plant life. The appellate body agreed, stating that the U.S. could, under WTO rules, adopt restrictions in order to protect the environment, but said that it had failed to impose its ban in a nondiscriminatory manner. Because the issue is so difficult and pits developed against developing nations, Director-General Ruggiero called for the establishment of an international framework to define the relationship between environmental agreements and the WTO objective of promoting trade. In his opinion, "asking the WTO to solve issues which are not central to its work, especially when these are issues which governments have failed to address satisfactorily in other contexts, is not just a recipe for failure, it could do untold harm to the trading system itself." Mr. Ruggiero's frustration is understandable, but it is misplaced. Environmental problems are as international as trade itself. If international standards are not developed by the WTO, then national standards can be used to protect not just the environment, but local markets as well.

Computer

This dispute was between the U.S. and the EU and involved trade worth $2.5 billion. In 1994, the EU decided to reduce tariffs on data processing equipment, including computer equipment. Later in the year, however, Ireland and the United Kingdom decided to reclassify Local Area Network (LAN) equipment as telecommunications equipment. In 1995, the EU followed suit. A LAN interconnects a number of computers and computer peripherals using a cabling system. These cables allow for the flow of data from one device to the other. The effect of the reclassification was to double the applicable import tariff on LANs. The U.S. filed a complaint arguing that this was a violation of Article II.1 of the GATT. In February 1998, the WTO dispute settlement panel upheld the U.S. complaint. However, the EU decided to appeal the decision, and the WTO appellate body favored the EU position. Meanwhile, EU trade in LANs had doubled.

Future

Few international organizations have as much potential to harmonize world trade as the WTO. Its membership is broad-based, and is steadily increasing the trade sectors under negotiation. But the WTO is facing a series of "choice points" that could influence its long-term success. Among these are the replacement of its first director-general, institutional reform, the accession of new members, and the prospect of more sectorial agreements or a new "round" of trade negotiations or both. Any one of these changes, and far more the lot of them, could have a profound impact on the future of world trade. For, if progress falters at the multinational level, regional trading groups are almost certain to develop their own standards, competing with the WTO.

Leadership Succession

The selection of the first WTO Director General took three months because each of the three major trading blocs (the EU, Japan and the Americas) put forward a different candidate. When the U.S. candidate (former Mexican president Salinas) was discredited, consensus formed around Renato Ruggiero, a former Italian minister and businessman. The U.S. reluctantly agreed to his appointment, but only if he would step down after one four-year term (April 1999), not to be succeeded by a European. Whomever succeed him (there were four nominees, again by region; Hassan Abouyoub of Morocco, Roy MacLaren of Canada, Mike Moore of New Zealand, and Supachai Panitchpakid of Thailand) had his work cut out for him. For Mr. Ruggiero proved to be an extraordinarily effective leader, insisting that the terms of the GATT be adhered to and pushing sectorial negotiations, but shrewd enough to know that the GATT is a political as well as legal document, requiring some forgiveness when the trade liberalization pace set by some nations, or the treaty itself, cannot be met by others. His deft balancing of the competing pressures of international trade has given the WTO tremendous credibility and produced about as much trade harmony as could be expected in four short years. At the same time, he broadened the reach of the WTO, insisting that leading traders make concessions for the world's poorest countries and that the concerns of nongovernmental organizations (NGOs) be taken into consideration in setting trade policy. From a global trade standpoint, Ruggiero was a brilliant first choice to head the WTO. The selection of his successor was to be something of a referendum on his strong, practical leadership. Will developing nations support another director general who so transparently favors a Western, capitalist approach? Will the world's industrialized nations trust a second-tier trading nation (which hold over one-half of WTO seats) to lead so important an institution? Should the WTO directorate be highly legalistic, or more conciliatory?

Institutional Reform

A second challenge to the WTO is to reform its dispute resolution process. Its critics claim that it needs to be made more participatory (at present, only WTO members can initiate and prosecute complaints), transparent (the proceedings are private) and speedier (the average proceeding takes about 34 months to complete). Reform suggestions have been submitted by a number of WTO members, including Japan, the EU and the U.S. "Substantive talks" began in October 1998 but are not expected to conclude until sometime in 1999. If that schedule is adhered to, then improvements in the process might be adopted at the next ministerial meeting or round of negotiations. Meanwhile, those parties that feel that they did not get "justice" in the WTO process (for example, Kodak in the Fuji film case) or that won their case but had difficulty enforcing the decision (the U.S. in the hormone and banana disputes) may resort to unilateral retaliation (allowed under GATT rules).

This will put even greater pressure on the WTO to reform, but it may also polarize its membership. A number of WTO members, particularly those with weak economies, say they are threatened not aided by strong enforcement mechanisms and rapid market openings. These nations are more numerous than industrialized WTO states and may react negatively to persistent pressure from the latter to strengthen enforcement devices. Any change is likely to strengthen, not weaken, the WTO enforcement mechanism legally. But one has to remember that there was no true enforcement mechanism prior to the WTO. It is almost certain to be improved soon, for experience has shown that reform is needed. But it would be a shame if a multilateral system with great potential was abandoned for unilateral methods that would be divisive and probably no more successful.

Expanding WTO Membership

There is a long queue to join the WT O, for membership gives a nation status and a voice in today's trading world. Membership also gives nations the right to enforce GATT terms against other members, although it carries the reciprocal duty to obey them.

Two of the world's largest trading nations China and Russia remain outside. Until they can be absorbed into a global trading system, the WTO will not have the scope or the influence it needs to be a complete success. And yet the economic problems in China and Russia may be so large and fundamental that there is no way of finessing their WTO membership. Until the Russian leadership is stable enough and the Chinese leadership cooperative enough to allow them to join the WTO, perhaps it is better that they be excluded. This is destabilizing in itself. But, as the 1990s ended, Russia seemed to be drifting farther away from rather than closer to WTO membership and China was making only modest progress.

Millennium Round

The last major challenge facing the WTO is whether to begin a new "round" of trade negotiations around the year 2000. That seems likely. Although the Uruguay Round was long (eight years), difficult and exhausting, it was undoubtably the best round ever. Perhaps the negotiators learned something from it or forgot what an ordeal it was. Most probably, the agreement on a new round reflects the fact that the sectoral agreements negotiated since the end of the Uruguay Round did not allow most WTO members much influence. If the U.S. and EU can agree to terms, the other nations pretty well have to go along. They would have more influence in a full round. Besides, a long agenda is building up in the WTO, from agriculture to foreign investment to competition policy. Not all of these can be addressed speedily in sectorial negations. But neither does a new round exclude sectorial talks.

In such economically and politically sensitive areas as environmental protection, human rights and state aid, WTO member countries differ considerably in their traditions and abilities to conform to a global standard. While human rights may be of great concern to the U.S. and other developed nations, the subject is of less concern to developing countries that are eager to improve their economies by any means possible and depend heavily on human labor. The WTO can move forward only with the consensus of a majority of its members. To assume that there is an American answer for every situation is a non-starter. While saving sea turtles may be of utmost importance to us, it is less concern to third-world fishermen struggling to make a living. Because such differences are somewhat subjective and not central to trade as such, they may lend themselves to more voluntary agreements than to WTO negotiations.

WTO Director General Ruggiero recently argued that involving the WTO in environmental issues is "asking to solve issues which are not central to its work." On the other hand, the WTO is emerging as the last, best resort for an enormous range of trade and social concerns that eventually must be handled at the multinational level.

11

Mechanism for Dispute Resolution by WTO

Introduction

The most significant improvement of the WTO over the GATT 1947 is its dispute settlement understanding (DSU). The GATT clauses for trade disputes settlement were too vague and too brief: contained in three precious paragraphs. The DSU, spelled out in 40 pages, incorporates several new dimensions such as the role of rules that cannot be vetoed by a single member country, clear schedules and time-bound actions in processing disputes and their effective compliance, recognition of the role of customary international public law and provision of measures to compensate members for adverse impacts of any trade policy violation by one or more measures. The DSU was expected to contribute toward security and predictability to the multilateral trading systems.

During the first four years of existence of the new DSU, the complaints by developed country members added to 124 requests dealing with 96 different subjects. Complaints by developing country members during this period were 31 requests, dealing with 29 different subjects. There were 4 complaints by both developed and developing country members with 10 requests these included three requests made by developed country members. The total number of consultation requests made by developing country member was 40; on the basis of distinct matters, the number was 32.

The role of the global trading institutions and specifically that of the WTO is critical as well in this context. The US has been the most active litigant, both in filing cases against other members and in defending various cases filed against it. Some of the cases are rather insignificant in the context of global trade volumes affected or potentially to be affected, but the dispute is one of the compliance with agreed upon principles of trade and various rules evolved under the WTO Agreement. For example, five cases were filed a few months ago by the US against Belgium, France, Greece, Ireland and the Netherlands; all these relate to income tax subsidies, apparently in possible violation of the agreements on subsidies inhibiting competitiveness of exports. In the case against Belgium, this involved the provision of tax rules which enabled corporate tax payers to receive special tax exemption for recruiting personnel with export related work functions.

This chapter highlights some of the important features of the DSU, and practical cases dealing especially with an interface of trade and environmental agreements. Appendix I summarizes the dispute settlement time table laid out under the DSU. One of the detailed case studies deals with the 8-year long US-EU banana dispute, given in Appendix II. Although this case does not fall under trade environment disputes, the practical working of the GATT/WTO systems is elucidated with this illustration. Lessons of experience in this regard are particularly useful if the environmental trade measures possess an element of urgency and/or irreversibility.

Legal foundations for dispute resolution

GATT Articles I (MFN), III (national treatment of 'like products'), and XI (limitations on the use of non-tariff barriers) are among the most significant provisions which could conflict with some of the proposed ETMs initiated at country level. These measures are generally handled at the multilateral level rather than unilateral levels. None of the three articles mentioned above warrants any significant changes in order to accommodate environmental considerations.

The original GATT process for dispute resolution had very little merit in its approaches and much less in dealing with any environmental trade measure-related disputes. Lack of provisions regarding the environment, coupled with almost total non-existence of environmental expertise on the GATT panels precipitated a series of rulings which were very narrow in their interpretation; most did not stretch beyond the interpretation of the words of the GATT Articles, possibly in a contextual manner. As Jackson pointed, the flaws of the GATT dispute resolution process originated in the 'birth defects', including the 'sparse language with little detail about goals or procedures', and 'fragmented settlement procedures'. The DSU under WTO established a unified dispute settlement system for all parts of the GATT/WTO system. The WTO Agreement contains the Rules and Procedures Governing the Settlement of Disputes; some of the important schedules of disputes settlement process and the transmission of information for resolution of disputes. Two key WTO Articles of Agreement state:

1. Article XVI.1: 'the WTO shall be guided by the decisions, procedures and customary practices followed by the Contracting Parties to GATT 1947'.
2. Article XVI.3: 'In the event of a conflict between a provision of this Agreement and a provision of any of the Multilateral Trade Agreements, the provision of this Agreement shall prevail to the extent of conflict.'

The WTO dispute settlement stated in Article 3.2 of the DSU that the disputes will be resolved in accordance with 'customary rules of interpretation of public international law'. The GATT provisions and its environmental exceptions Article XX remain largely in tact under the new GATT 1994; several features of the role, merits and limitations of these provisions are relevant here. Besides, the overarching WTO Articles of Agreement, and other important Agreements like SPS, SCM, TBT and their interdependent interpretations constitute the legal bases for resolution of trade/trade-environment disputes under the WTO system.

The Dispute Settlement Body (DSB) of the WTO is the apex level group to offer a ruling on all trade disputes of the members. The DSU of the WTO, agreed by all the member countries of the world body states in its Article 21.1: 'Prompt compliance with recommendations or rulings of the DSB is essential in order to ensure effective resolution of disputes to the benefit of all Members.' The

DSU was officially declared by the members as a 'central element in providing security and predictability to the multilateral trading systems'. According to the DSU, there is an obligation to perform and comply on behalf of the lost defendant in any dispute.

Article 16 of the DSU prevents blockage by a single member the DSB's acceptance of a panel report on any trade dispute. A panel report on a dispute will be deemed adopted unless there exists a consensus against it. This is called 'reverse consensus', a feature that constitutes a major improvement over the corresponding feature under the GATT mechanisms for dispute settlement. Unless a disputant opts to appeal, the panel report is submitted to the DSB for its consideration; the report is automatically adopted unless rejected by a consensus of the DSB. Appeals are permitted and can last up to 90 days. As pointed out in Jackson, a separate set of procedures for handling 'violation' and 'non violation' cases is incorporated for the first time for a treaty text.

Jackson summarized the operative parts of the DSU: the DSU establishes a preference for an obligation to perform the recommendation; indicates that compensation shall be required if the immediate withdrawal of the offending measures is infeasible or a non-event; and provides that in non violation cases, there exists no obligation to withdraw a disputed action, with an implication that in violation cases there exists an obligation to perform.

There has been a widely held view that the WTO mechanisms for dispute settlement are more legalistic than most other similar international institutions. However, the founding members, especially Canada, EC, and the US were in favour of such a system with the intention of devising effective transparent methods of dispute resolution and averting any global effects of uncertainties in the trading regimes. The DSU in its Article 3.7 states that a 'solution mutually acceptable to the parties to a dispute and consistent with the covered agreements is clearly to be preferred (over the use of panel procedures)'. However, some parties tend to ignore this principle of wisdom and seek to test the workability of legal and institutional arrangements.

The next section summarizes a set of trade-related environmental disputes processed under the GATT/WTO systems during the past few years. As in any case law, the original legal provisions are then illuminated in the application of the law. Lessons of experience are useful for appropriate legal reforms and any revisions in the original articles of agreement.

Trade-related environmental disputes in GATT/WTO

GATT hardly gained, nor even claimed any effective integration of trade policies and environmental considerations. Even after the 1992 UN Conference on Environment and Development (Rio Conference), it was clarified: the GATT's competence was limited to trade policies and those trade-related aspects of environmental policies which might result in significant trade effects for GATT contracting parties. In respect neither of its vocation nor of its competence was the GATT equipped to become involved in the tasks of reviewing national environmental priorities, setting environmental standards or developing global policies on the environment.

The narrow focus of the GATT mandate effectively precluded the incorporation of MEAs in trade polices. It is ironical that despite such a background under the GATT regime, a recent statement of the WTO Director General seeks environmental measures be the concern of the MEAs and would rather let WTO keep defending liberalized trade policies for their own sake. Under the GATT, six panel proceedings involving an examination of environmental measures or human health-related measures under Article XX were completed. Of the six reports, three have not been adopted. Under the WTO DSU, two such proceedings have been completed. The following provides a factual overview of a select set of these disputes, based on the document WTO.

1. Canada – Measures Affecting Exports of Unprocessed Herring and Salmon, adopted on 22 March 1988

Canada maintained that under its 1976 Canadian Fisheries Act, regulations prohibiting the exportation or sale for export of certain unprocessed herring and salmon. The US complained that these measures were inconsistent with GATT Article XI. Canada maintained that these export restrictions were part of a system of fishery resource management aimed at preserving fishery stocks, and hence justified under Article XX(g).The GATT Panel found that the measures maintained by Canada were contrary to GATT Article XI:1 and were justified neither by Article XI:2(b) nor by Article XX(g).

2. Thailand – Restrictions on Importation of and Internal Taxes on Cigarettes, adopted on 7 November 1990

Under its 1966 Tobacco Act, Thailand prohibited the importation of cigarettes and other tobacco preparations, but authorized the sale of domestic cigarettes. Besides, cigarettes were subject to an excise tax, a business tax and a municipal tax. The United States complained that the import restrictions were inconsistent with GATT Article XI:1, and considered that they were not justified by Article XI:2(c), nor by Article XX(b). The United States also requested the Panel to find that the internal taxes were inconsistent with GATT Article III:2. Thailand argued that the import restrictions were justified under Article XX(b) because the government had adopted measures which could only be effective if cigarettes imports were prohibited and because chemicals and other additives contained in US cigarettes might make them more harmful than Thai cigarettes. The Panel found that the import restrictions were inconsistent with Article XI:1 and not justified under Article XI:2(c). It further concluded that the import restrictions were not 'necessary' within the meaning of Article XX(b). The internal taxes were, however, found to be consistent with GATT Article III:2.

3 United States – Taxes on Automobiles, not adopted, circulated on 11 October 1994

Three US measures on automobiles were under scrutiny: the luxury tax on automobiles ('luxury tax'), the gas guzzler tax on automobiles ('gas guzzler'), and the Corporate Average Fuel Economy (CAFE) regulation. The European Community complained that these measures were inconsistent with GATT Article III and could not be justified under Article XX(g) or (d).

The Panel found that both the luxury tax which applied to cars sold for over $30,000 and the gas guzzler tax which applied to the sale of automobiles attaining less than 22.5 miles per gallon (m.p.g) were consistent with Article III:2 of GATT.

The CAFE regulation required the average fuel economy for passenger cars manufactured in the US or sold by any importer not to fall below 27.5m.p.g. Companies that were both importers and domestic manufacturers had to assess average fuel economy separately for imported passenger automobiles and for those manufactured domestically. During the first month of operation of the WTO, Venezuela complained to the DSB that the US was using discriminatory trade rules against gasoline imports. A year later the dispute panel completed its report. The panel and the DSB ruled that the US policy violated 'national treatment' provision under GATT and the GATT Article XX does not apply. The Panel found the CAFE regulation to be inconsistent with GATT Article III:4 because the separate foreign fleet accounting system discriminated against foreign cars and the fleet averaging differentiated between imported and domestic cars on the basis of factors relating to control or ownership of producers or importers, and not on the basis of factors directly related to the products as such. The Panel also found that the separate foreign fleet accounting was not justified under Article XX(g). The Panel found that the CAFE regulation could not be justified under Article XX(d). The US agreed and amended its regulations at the end of the implementation period in August 1997.

4. United States — Import Prohibition of Certain Shrimp and Shrimp Products, adopted on 6 November 1998

Seven species of sea turtles exist with their habitats distributed around the world in subtropical and tropical areas. Sea turtles have been adversely affected by their harvesting and also incidental capture in fisheries, destruction of their habitats, pollution of the oceans. In early 1997, India, Malaysia, Pakistan and Thailand brought a joint complaint against a ban imposed by the US on the importation of certain shrimp and shrimp products.

The US Endangered Species Act of 1973 (ESA) listed as endangered or threatened the five species of sea turtles that occur in US waters and prohibited their harvesting within the US, in its territorial sea and the high seas. Also, the US required that US shrimp trawlers use 'turtle excluder devices' (TEDs) in their nets when fishing in areas where there is a significant likelihood of encountering sea turtles. In practice, countries having any of the five species of sea turtles within their jurisdiction and harvesting shrimp with mechanical means had to impose on their fishermen requirements comparable to those borne by US fisherman in the shrimp harvesting activity, mainly to use of TEDs at all times, if they sought to be certified and need market access to export shrimp products to the US.

The Panel considered that the ban imposed by the US was inconsistent with GATT Article XI and could not be justified under

GATT Article XX. The Appellate Body found that the measure qualified for provisional justification under Article XX(g), but failed to meet the requirements of the chapeau of Article XX, and was not justified under Article XX of GATT 1994. One of the most significant and comprehensive analyses of environmental trade disputes relates to the tuna-dolphin issue.

Tuna-Dolphin Dispute

The tuna-dolphin case still attracts considerable attention because of its implications for environmental disputes. It was handled under the old GATT dispute settlement procedure. Tuna often swim beneath schools of dolphins. When tuna is harvested with purse seine nets, dolphins are trapped in the nets. They often die unless they are released. The USMMPA sets dolphin protection standards for the domestic American fishing fleet and for countries whose fishing boats catch yellow fin tuna in that part of the Pacific Ocean. If a country exporting tuna to the United States cannot prove to US authorities that it meets the dolphin-safe standards set out in the US law, the US government must embargo imports of the fish from that country. In this dispute, Mexico was the exporting country concerned. Its exports of tuna to the US were banned. Mexico complained in 1991 under the GATT dispute settlement procedure. Tuna-Dolphin I: United States Restrictions on the Imports of Tuna, not adopted, circulated on 3 September 1991.

The MMPA required a general prohibition of the 'taking' (harassment, hunting, capture, killing or attempt thereof) and importation into the US of marine mammals, except with explicit authorization. It governed, in particular, the taking of marine mammals incidental to harvesting yellow fin tuna in the Eastern Tropical Pacific Ocean (ETP), an area where dolphins are known to swim above schools of tuna. Under the MMPA, the import of commercial fish (or fish products) which have been caught with commercial fishing technology which results in the incidental kill or incidental serious injury of ocean mammals in excess of US standards were prohibited. Imports of tuna from countries purchasing tuna from a country subject to the primary nation embargo are also prohibited (intermediary nation embargo). Mexico claimed that the import prohibition on yellow fin tuna and tuna products was inconsistent with Articles XI, XIII and III of GATT. The US maintained that the direct embargo was consistent with Article III and, in the alternative, was covered by Articles XX(b) and XX(g). The US also argued that the intermediary nation embargo was consistent with Article III and, in the alternative, was justified by Article XX (b), (d) and (g).The Panel found that the import prohibition under the direct and the intermediary embargoes did not constitute internal regulations within the meaning of Article III, was inconsistent with Article XI:1 and also not justified by Article XX paragraphs (b) and (g). Also, the intermediary embargo was not justified under Article XX(d). Mexico requested constitution of a panel in February 1991. A number of 'intermediary' countries also expressed their interest in the dispute. The panel reported to GATT parties in September 1991. It concluded:

- that the US could not embargo imports of tuna products from Mexico simply because Mexican regulations on the way tuna was produced did not satisfy US regulations. The panel's objection to process versus product distinction is clear;
- that GATT rules did not allow one country to take trade action for the purpose of attempting to enforce its own domestic laws in another country even to protect animal health or exhaustible natural resources. The term used here is 'extra-territoriality'.

The US embargo was aimed at regulating not the sale of a product, but rather its process of production (the mode of harvesting in this case). Under GATT rules, the panel argued, the US was obliged to provide Mexican tuna (as a product) with a treatment no less favorable to that accorded to US tuna (also as a product), regardless of how the tuna itself was harvested. The panel also observed that whilst GATT Contracting Parties could adopt GATT-inconsistent measures, categorized under the 'General Exceptions' provision of GATT Article XX for the protection of the environment or the conservation of exhaustible natural resources, it was not clearly spelled out in the Agreement whether the resources being protected could fall outside the jurisdiction of the Party adopting the environmental controls. The dispute did not end here. The new phase followed with a new complaint, described below.

Restrictions of the imports of Tuna

The EEC and the Netherlands complained that both the primary and the intermediary nation embargoes, enforced pursuant to the MMPA did not fall under Article III, were inconsistent with Article XI:1 and were not covered by any of] the exceptions of Article XX. The US considered that the intermediary nation embargo was consistent with GATT since it was covered by Article XXI, paragraphs (g), (b) and (d), and that the primary nation embargo did not nullify or impair any benefits accruing to the EEC or the Netherlands since it did not apply to these countries. The embargo also applied to 'intermediary' countries handling the tuna en route from Mexico to the United States. Often the tuna is processed and packed in one of these countries. In this dispute, the 'intermediary' countries facing the embargo were Costa Rica, Italy, Japan and Spain, and earlier France, the Netherlands Antilles, and the United Kingdom. Others, including Canada, Colombia, and the Republic of Korea, and members of the Association of the Southeast Asian Nations, were also named as intermediaries.

The Panel found that neither the primary nor the intermediary nation embargo were covered under Article III, that both were contrary to Article XI: I and not covered by the exceptions in Article XX (b), (g) or (d) of the GATT. It was generally felt that if the US arguments were accepted, then any country could ban imports of a product from another country merely because the exporting country has different environmental, health and social policies from its own. It was opined that this could lead to a possible 'flood of protectionist abuses', and conflict with the main purpose of the multilateral trading system, that is, achieve predictability through trade rules.

The panel's conclusion that another international treaty the CITES would be relevant to the interpretation of a GATT provision only when the treaty was ratified by all GATT parties does not appear to be consistent with Article 31 (3) (c) of the Vienna Convention on the Law of Treaties, argued Palmeter and Mavroidis . This Convention states that 'any relevant rules of international law applicable in the relations between the parties' shall be taken into account in a dispute resolution. Article 30 of the Vienna Convention is important in the application of MEAs. Article 30 (3) states that when the disputing countries are signatories of two agreements, the later in time prevails.

Also, Article 30 (4) (b) specifies that, as between a state party to both treaties and a state party to only one of the treaties, the treaty to which both are parties becomes binding. As explained in Palmeter and Mavroidis , this means that, in the event that a WTO member is a signatory to an MEA and another member is not, the MEA could not affect the rights and obligations under the WTO Articles of Agreement: 'a treaty binds only the contracting parties and neither rights nor duties arise under a treaty for a state not a party'.

The GATT 1991 Panel deployed rather feeble and 'dubious reasoning' in its interpretation of GATT Article XX(g), as explained by Chang:

It pointed to a previous GATT Panel's position that a trade measure must be 'primarily aimed at rendering effective' the 'restrictions on domestic production or consumption' in order to be 'made effective in conjunction with' those restrictions. The Panel asserted that a 'country can effectively control the production or consumption of an exhaustible natural resource only to the extent that the production or consumption is under its jurisdiction' and concluded that 'Article XX(g) was intended to permit contracting parties to take trade measures primarily aimed at rendering effective restrictions on production or consumption within their jurisdiction.' It is important to note that the GATT Panel decision ensured the compatibility of restrictions with the purpose of the trade measure and not its effectiveness. The GATT 1991 Panel decision with reference to interpretation of 'effective' measures is neither supported by the text of the Article XX(g) nor by the position of the previous panel it cites.

Also, as stated by Esty, the major lacuna with Article XX is that 'it makes the legitimacy of environmental regulation turn on what is produced, not how it is produced'. The irrational rigidity in seeking compliance with neutrality toward PPM continues to plague the GATT provisions in so far as these cannot contribute toward harmonization of trade and environmental policies.

Toward Improved Methods

GATT Article III mandates national treatment of 'like products': it requires that imports from the territory of any contracting party 'be accorded treatment no less favorable than that accorded to like products of national origin in respect to all laws, regulations and requirements affecting their internal sale'. This requirement that all like products be treated equally limits the flexibility of a country to differentiate on the basis of environmental impact of products (during their life-cycle or different stages of production and usage). If the provision of the Article allows for comparison of 'like products' in terms of their environmental effects, we enter into the arena of differentiation on the basis of process and production methods as well. It is widely feared that such a distinction could allow some of the countries to utilize the provision to bring about disguised non tariff barriers in the name of the environmental features underlying the products. It is likely that some cases could arise, but this problem is minimized when the basis of restriction is sought to be scientific and transparent guidelines are issued by the WTO for this purpose. A meaningful provision of process and product methods, with a slight modification of Article XX and/or Article XI should largely serve the purpose of integrating environmental considerations into trade issues. The inertia of some of the organizations or members should not be allowed to cost the economy-environment integration at the global and regional levels.

TRIPS regulates process and production methods (PPM): if a producer in a TRIPS member country resorts to patented production methods without obeying the appropriate international patent laws and exports such products to other member countries, an importing country could take 'appropriate measures' to prohibit such imports. As suggested in Fletcher, a differentiation on the basis of production methods already found its origin under the TRIPS agreement, and an extension of similar reasoning to ecodumping would make sense. The latter could build on the provisions of antidumping and TRIPS to accommodate environmental aspects of trade.

To recognize the experience and perspectives of the Tuna-Dolphin Panel II of 1994, it is important to delineate a three step analysis to determine the applicability of environmental exceptions provided under GATT Article XX(b). These involve the determination of the following: 1. whether the policies in question are really designed to 'protect human, animal, or plant life'; 2. whether these are 'necessary' for the stated objective; 3. whether the measures lead to an arbitrary or unjustifiable discrimination between countries where similar conditions prevail. The Panel stated that the eligibility of trade measures 'necessary' was allowed only when other less GATT inconsistent measures were exhausted. Logically, a panel can usually come with an unexploited measure as potential candidate for rejecting any application of 'necessary' measures. When environmental considerations are important, such a ranking of alternatives can ignore the merits of these considerations and weigh the merits of alternatives simply in terms of their GATT-consistency or selection of the least GATT-inconsistent measure. These hazards can be avoided when the trade measures are evaluated with reference to GATT provision which is still lacking that allows a comprehensive economic and environmental impact assessment of proposed ETMs, while maintaining the main principles of non-discrimination. Under the new proposal, an evaluation of an ETM is based on a weighted index of agreed upon objectives, follows an agreed pattern of PPM differentiation and other guidelines of adoption.

GATT Panel decisions are reflective of the position in the preamble to the GATT Articles, which states that GATT is meant to facilitate the 'full use of the natural resources of the world'. Let us note that this prescription is vastly different from a required 'optimum' use of natural resources (leaving aside, for a moment, alternate definitions and premises for optimum use). A full use scenario is more like that of 'there is no tomorrow', and is built on the disparate high discounting of future. A number of limitations in the useful applications of the GATT Articles arose from such background. GATT Panels have clearly refused to recognize the application of provisions of various MEAs.

Under the GATT/WTO, DSB does not consider obligations of members under MEAs even when both disputants ratified the competing or complementing treaty, as was amplified in the TunaDolphin 1994 Panel Report. The Panel refused to consider any obligations under CITES or other MEAs. The Panel cited Article 31 of the Vienna Convention with a possible misinterpretation of the requirement that all parties must have been signatories of both the agreements (GATT as well as an MEA like CITES). The reference here to 'all parties' should have been all disputants and not all signatories of all agreements under consideration for dispute resolution. Finally, it is important that the new GATT 1994 and the

DSU recognize the prescriptions of the preamble to the WTO charter wherein the roles of the need to protect the environment, and the need for sustainable development are clearly stated. It remains an empty foundation if these aspects are not fully integrated into the DSU and its methods of dispute resolution.

12

Toward a Better Future

Introduction

If the sole objective of a multilateral trade regime is to ensure smooth and predictable functioning of the global trade activities, with little regard for the interlinks with environmental sustainability, the trade system will not continue to remain smooth nor predictable. The role of information and institutions is very significant in mitigating potential problems.

The operational objectives of multilateral trading system need to be formulated in terms of market institutions and their governance. The issue of governance must be better appreciated in terms of the implications on transaction costs, comprising mainly the costs of undertaking trade transactions as well as the costs of devising institutional arrangements, monitoring and enforcement. The role of welfare enhancing competition policies on a fair and non-discriminatory basis remains the foundation for all approaches toward multilateral trade governance. The natural forces operating on the market institutions constitute the fundamental dynamics, and these can only be partially influenced by the rules of governance. At the crux of the matter remains the issue of 'contestability of markets' for a detailed account of the features). This feature may be characterized in terms of the prevalence of market conditions of the competitive processes wherein the anticompetitive forces due to government or private actions are eliminated so as to ensure unimpeded market access.

The primary role of the WTO may be viewed in terms of its effective contribution to the creation and sustenance of international contestability of markets. This characterization remains invariant under its obligations to ensure sustainable trading patterns and contribute sustainable development processes with an integration of trade-environment-development issues. The WTO rules should attempt to protect the competitiveness of the global markets, and not necessarily the competitors. In other words, protecting the competitors does not usually amount to ensuring the workability of contestable competitive markets. The main reason for this process is built on the dynamic effects and externalities of such protective devices, direct or indirect. As long as the institutions are appropriately devised and sustained to govern the multilateral trading systems, the operative rules apply at each time instant to ensure that any deviations built over time (possibly as a result of one or more specific interventions) are brought in line for conformity.

Another important feature of international trade, not fully recognized in the WTO framework relates to the role of implicit trade barriers posed by large conglomerates and cartels with monopolistic powers to alter the competitiveness of various markets. Some of the rules under the WTO address these concerns: Article VIII of the GATS stipulates that member countries should ensure that their monopolistic enterprises do not exercise undue market influence. Similarly, Section 8 of the TRIPS Agreement provides measures against anticompetitive practices in contractual licenses. The role of an international antitrust code remains an issue for further consideration within the WTO framework. This should be seen as an element of the need to ensure international contestability of markets.

The role of multilateral trade mechanisms should also be to address some of the issues of global economic inequities and their continuous deterioration. According to a recent assessment of the WTO, the global market factors, domestic political and economic crises in some of the developing countries, and the financial crises magnified by debt crises and exchange rate crises led to force down the share of primary products in the global trade of all goods to a share of 20 per cent. Let us recognize that the primary product producers are largely the countries in the least developed and developing categories. The result of global economic integration should not be allowed to deteriorate itself to contribute to some of these problems. The products share constituted the lowest level of the share since the end of World War II. Similarly, the value of traded goods declined for that year by two percent despite a growth in the volume of traded goods by about 3.5 per cent. Such factors, combined with ever increasing debt levels for developing countries, particularly debt servicing ratios to exports, do not suggest the formation of the most appropriate foundations for the functioning of an efficient global market. This market heavily constrained and not a 'free market' by any measure. A reasonably comprehensive analysis of the structure and functioning of the global trade systems would reveal the relative roles of various interlocking systems. It is useful to realize the contributory roles of constrained exports at largely pre-determined levels based on debt service requirements to fulfill continued credit access from global financial institutions for indebted countries, even under depressed 'market' prices and exchange rates. Attempts to devise and apply market principles without due recognition of the institutional factors can lead to misleading and unwise prescriptions for the vulnerable.

Let us recall an observation of Paul Samuelson: free trade will not necessarily maximize the real income or consumption and utility possibilities of any one country; winners can potentially contribute to losers and gain from trade. An analogous extension holds good when we include the implications of trade gains for the environment. The operational implications is that gains from trade should be partly made available to offset the negative environmental impacts.

It is by no means less important that the multilateral trade system takes into account humane considerations, social dimensions of production and trade activities, the moral basis of trade expansion and protection of the vulnerable, be it the environment, or the poor working populations, the rights of humans and other living species. Indifference or insensitivity to some of these values tends to perpetuate a cycle of mutual exploitation and disrupt the natural cohesion of various systems. Material welfare is but a component of the determinants of human welfare. The role of trade fits into such a framework usually as a means of economic prosperity rather than pretend as an end product by itself. Accordingly, it is necessary that an integrated approach to trade issues is developed. It is apt to quote Theodore Roosevelt in this context. In his 1937 address to the US Congress President Roosevelt stated: 'Goods produced under conditions that do not meet a rudimentary standard of decency should be regarded as contraband and not allowed to pollute the channels of international commerce'. This prescription remains robustly valid today just as it was relevant several decades ago.

Institutions for sustainable trade and development

The WTO came into existence with a unique institutional configuration; it needs an effective institutional constellation, however. This is better achieved in both horizontal and vertical coordination with global institutions and stakeholders. The role of the WTO members remains the key to its effective contribution, but the role of its demarcated Committees and other working groups is of great importance as well. Given the initial base and platform with legal structure, the WTO is expected to contribute significantly toward fair and sustainable trade. The role of the regional trading arrangements remains important, but efforts should be made to ensure that these arrangements also synchronize with the objectives of the WTO framework.

The role of terms of trade in the broad patterns affecting the developing countries is unlikely to be a useful weakness for the global economies, given the features of their interdependence. The financial institutions should devise sustainable policies in various sectors and regions so that economic integration is achieved on a sustainable basis. It is useful to recognize that global economic integration does imply global environmental integration as well. Thus, there exists little rationale for devising economic or other policies which maintain neutrality to various environmental interdependencies across different societies, economies and time intervals. The degree of endogeneity of the state of the environment is directly affected by the 'quality' as well as quantity characteristics of trade and other transactions. Greater recognition of these issues and provision of rather comprehensive instruments to modulate the effects will be a globally useful activity for the WTO.

The need for greater use of environmental knowledge, possibly with an active cooperation with the Intergovernmental Panel on Climate Change (IPCC), UNEP, FAO, and other internationally recognized scientific institutions will be a useful additional input into the decision making processes in the WTO systems. It is not entirely valid to maintain that any in-depth assessment would mean duplication of work of other institutions in the international network; none of these have a comparable charter and multilateral obligations to fulfill, and most do not have an active an active (or in principle active, as per the charter) membership role in formulating policies. This feature should be utilized as a strength for the institution and its effectiveness. Cooperation with institutions like the World Bank and IMF is desirable, but their mandate is entirely different. There are no 'client states' and shareholders for the WTO, but the business of the financial institutions is in terms of its clientele and shareholders. The issue of accountability is thus divergent as well. The WTO has a unique opportunity to contribute harmonious and sustainable development of the global systems. A recognition and contribution in this direction is a reasonable expectation for the WTO to fulfill.

Bibliography

Allen D. (1979), "'Tariff Games'", in S. Brams, A. Schotter, and G. Schwoediauer (eds.), "Applied Game Theory" (Wuerzburg: Physica-Verlag).

Anderson K. (1992), "'Effects on the Environment and Welfare of Liberalizing World Trade: The Cases of Coal and Food'", in K. Anderson and R. Blackhurst (eds.), *The Greening of World Trade Issues* (London: Harvester-Wheatsheaf).

Banks G. (1983), "'The Economics and Politics of Countertrade'", *World Economy*, 6: 159-82.

Bhagwati J. (1971), "'The Generalized Theory of Distortions and Welfare'", in J. N. Bhagwati, R. Mundell, R. Jones, and J. Vanek (eds.), *Trade, Balance of Payments and Growth* (Amsterdam: North Holland).

Braga C. P. (1995), *'Trade-Related Intellectual Property Issues'*, in W. Martin and A. /> Winters (eds.), "The Uruguay Round and the Developing Economies" (Washington DC: World Bank, forthcoming).

Caves R. (1987), "'Industrial Policy and Trade Policy: The Connections'", in H. /> Kierzkowski (ed.), *Protection and Competition in International Trade* (London: Basil Blackwell).

Conybeare J. (1987), *Trade Wars* (Princeton, NJ: Princeton University Press).

Cooper R. (1988), *'Comment'* in L. Castle and C. Findlay (eds.), *Pacific Trade in Services* (London: Allen and Unwin).

Corden W. M. (1974), "Trade Policy and Economic Welfare" (Oxford: Clarendon Press).

Dam K. (1970), "The GATT. Law and International Economic Organization" (Chicago: University of Chicago Press).

Davies S. and McGuiness A. (1982), "'Dumping at less than Marginal Cost'", *Journal of International Economics*, 12: 169-82.

Downs A. (1954), "An Economic Theory of Democracy" (New York: Harper & Row).

Edwards S. and Savastano M. (1989), "'Latin America's Intra-Regional Trade: Evolution and Future'", in D. T. Greenaway, T. Hyclak, and R. Thornton (eds.), *Economic Aspects of Regional Trading Arrangements* (New York: New York University Press).

Eglin R. (1987), *'Surveillance of Balance-of-Payments Measures in the GATT', World Economy*, 10: 1-26.

Evans J. W. (1972), "The Kennedy Round in American Trade Policy" (Cambridge: Harvard University Press).

Feinberg R. and Kaplan S. (1993), *'Fishing Downstream: The Political Economy of Effective Protection', Canadian Journal of Economics*, 26: 150-58.

Feketekuty G. (1988), *International Trade in Services: An Overview and Blueprintfor Negotiations* (Cambridge Mass.: Ballinger Publications).

Garrett G. (1992), "'International Cooperation and Institutional Choice: The European Community's Internal Market'", *International Organization*, 46: 543-60.

Garten J. (1994), "'New Challenges in the World Economy: The Antidumping Law and US Trade Policy'", speech presented at the US Chamber of Commerce, Washington DC, 7 Apr.

Hamilton C. and Whalley J. (1989), "'Coalitions in the Uruguay Round'", *Weltwirtschaftliches Archiv*, 125: 547-62.

Herin J. (1986), *'Rules of Origin and Differences between Tariff Levels in EFTA and in the EC'*, Occasional Paper no. 13 (Geneva: EFTA).

Jacquemin A. (1994), ' "Goals and Means of European Antitrust Policy After 1992"', in H. Demsetz and A. Jacquemin (eds.), *Antitrust Economics: New Challenges for Competition Policy* (Lund: Lund University Press).

Kemp M. and Wan H. (1976), ' "An Elementary Proposition Concerning the Formation of Customs Unions"', *Journal of International Economics*, 6: 95-7.

Kindleberger C. (1983), ' "Standards as Public, Collective and Private Goods"', *Kyklos*, 36: 377-96.

Lawrence R. and Litan R. (1991), ' "The World Trading System After the Uruguay Round"', Boston *University International Law Journal*, 8: 247-76.

Leary V. (1994), ' "Worker's Rights and International Trade: The Social Clause"', in J. /> Bhagwati and R. Hudec (eds.), *Harmonization and Fair Trade: Prerequisite for Free Trade?* (Cambridge, Mass.: MIT Press, forthcoming).

McCloskey D. (1982), *The Applied Theory of Price* (New York: Macmillan).

McMillan J. (1993), ' "Does Regional Integration Foster Open Trade? Economic Theory and GATT's Article XXIV"', in K. Anderson and R. Blackhurst (eds.), *Regional Integration and the Global Trading System* (London: Harvester-Wheatsheaf).

OECD (Organization for Economic Cooperation and Development) (1993), *Industrial Policy in OECD Countries, Annual Review 1992* (Paris: OECD).

Palmeter N. D. (1995), ' "US Implementation of the Uruguay Round Antidumping Code"', *Journal of World Trade*, June.

Schott J. (1989) (ed.), *Free Trade Areas and US Trade Policy* (Washington D.C: Institute for International Economics). — — and Buurman J. (1994), *The Uruguay Round: An Assessment* (Washington DC: Institute for International Economics).

Sherwood R. (1990), *Intellectual Property and Economic Development* (Boulder, Colo.: Westview Press).

Tollison R. and Willett T. (1979), ' "An Economic Theory of Mutually Advantageous Issue Linkages in International Negotiations"', *International Organization*, 33: 42549.

Vaubel R. (1986), ' "A Public Choice Approach to International Organization"', *Public Choice*, 51: 39-57.

Vousden N. (1990), *The Economics of Trade Protection* (Cambridge: Cambridge University Press).

Weston A. (1994), ' "The Uruguay Round: Unraveling the Implications for the LeastDeveloped and Low-Income Countries"' (Geneva: UNCTAD).

Winham G. (1986), *International Trade and the Tokyo Round Negotiation* (Princeton, NJ: Princeton University Press).

Wonnacott R. (1991), *The Economics of Overlapping Free Trade Areas and the Mexican Challenge* (Toranto: C.D. Howe Institute).

World Bank (1986), *World Development Report* (Washington DC: World Bank). (1995), *Global Economic Prospects and the Developing Economies* (Washington DC: World Bank).

Xafa M., Kronenberg R., and Landell-Mills J. (1992), ' "The European Community's Trade and Trade-Related Industrial Policies"', *Working Paper no. 92/94* (Washington DC: International Monetary Fund).

Yang Y. (1994), ' "The Impact of Phasing out the MFA on World Clothing and Textile Markets"', *Journal of Development Studies*, 30: 892-915.

Index